East meets West

—a background to some Asian Faiths

Muhammad Iqbal

in collaboration with Dharam Kumar Vohra *and* Sardar Arjan Kirpal Singh
foreword by **David Lane**
Chairman, Commission for Racial Equality

Commission for Racial Equality,
Elliot House,
10/12 Allington Street,
London SW1E 5EH

September 1981

Cover design: Embroidery in gold thread on black velvet; designed by Alan Gaunt.

1st Edition 1970
2nd Edition 1973
3rd Edition 1981—revised

© M. Iqbal, D. K. Vohra, S. A. K. Singh & C. R. E.

ISBN 0 902355 94 5

Printed by: Regent (Printers) Limited, Queen Street South, Huddersfield HD1 3EU.
Telephone 0484 39331

CONTENTS

NOTES ON AUTHORS

Dr MUHAMMAD IQBAL, PhD MPhil CChem MRIC (London) BSc, Punjab University, Lahore. Former Chairman, Huddersfield Community Relations Council and founder of 'Home Tutor Scheme' teaching Asian ladies English. Member of the Yorkshire Water Authority, Leeds, and Home Secretary's Advisory Council on Race Relations, Home Office, London. Senior Lecturer in Chemistry and Adviser to Overseas Students at Huddersfield Polytechnic. Author of *The Call from the Minaret,* Hodder & Stoughton Educational. He has published widely on Race Relations and Religious Education.

Mr DHARAM KUMAR VOHRA, BA(Hons) MA, Punjab University. Specialist in Hindi, Urdu and Sanskrit languages. Police Liaison Officer, West Yorkshire Metropolitan Police (Bradford). Contributor to books on Hindu religion for schools.

SARDAR ARJAN KIRPAL SINGH, has been educated at British and American Universities, and holds qualifications in the multiple academic disciplines of Humanities, Education and Social Sciences. He has taught at all levels of education in Britain, as well as in American and Canadian Universities. Since 1950, he has been living in the UK and has made significant contributions in the fields of Community and Race Relations. His current research interests and fieldwork are focussed in the 'Sociology, Social Psychology, Phenomenology and Anthropology of Religion', with particular reference to the 'Sociology of Sikhism' and 'Sociolinguistics' of Religious language.

FOREWORD

There is a surfeit of books on world religions in the market. *East Meets West* is an addition but with a difference. Here is a brief resume of three faiths, Hinduism, Islam and Sikhism, represented mainly amongst ethnic minorities of the Asian extraction in the United Kingdom. Each section has been written by the follower of the faith thus combining facts with devotion that is manifest throughout the book. Where possible explanations of beliefs which generate practical encounters at places of work have been given in order to bring about understanding of and tolerance for the co-workers in industry, educational institutions and places of social intercourse. The Commission for Racial Equality has already published brief guideline papers on faiths and practices of Hindu, Muslim and Sikh workers for the benefit of employers. This publication provides in detail the information contained therein.

Social, cultural and educational disadvantage of ethnic minorities in multi-racial towns and cities compared with that of the community at large is not a new phenomenon. There has always been urban deprivation in the cross-section of the indigenous community. Accordingly, the Commission has published several research studies which lay great emphasis on making provisions within the normal resources, monetary and manpower, of government and local authority departments to incorporate in their programmes the specific needs of the ethnic minorities, to cater for urban deprivation and to promote inner-city development. This does not, however, preclude the necessity of special programmes for the benefit of ethnic minorities to fulfil the spirit and provision of the Race Relations Act 1976.

In this respect one may quote the value of teaching their mother tongues to the younger generation of the new settlers, which open up their religious scriptures and in additon would be helpful in retaining cultural indentity. With this in view the Commission has grant-aided some ethnic minority organisiations, thus helping them to undertake supplementary teaching and training for the ethnic minority school children in the evenings and or over the week-ends.

In addition, this publication argues at length such issues as the inclusion of these faiths in the school R.E., dress and dietary habits of children as well as adult believers. The last two chapters contain the respective calendars of festivals, their celebrations, customs and practices, making it clear for the benefit of the non-believers what is religious and what is purely social and cultural.

The publication will be found useful by teachers, community and social workers, health visitors, industrialists, police personnel, local and government officials who would like to seek information on different facets of the faiths of Hinduism, Islam and Sikhism. I am sure they will find it helpful in order to review their attitudes towards, and hence combat prejudice against, the followers of these faiths.

Finally, whilst the Commission for Racial Equality expresses its thanks to all three writers for their invaluable contributions, the views and opinions expressed are those of the contributors and not those of the Commission. Each contributor has been at liberty to express himself freely.

David Lane
Chairman
Commission for Racial Equality

INTRODUCTION

The belief in certain religious fundamentals makes a man a *Hindu,* a *Muslim,* or a *Sikh.* The belief in God is like a multi-pronged approach of different religions converging on the same 'Being'. However, it is the practice of their respective fundamentals, especially the rituals, that has, from time to time, caused problems for those at the shop-floor of British industry or at cross-contacts elsewhere in situations of work, recreation and entertainment.

Because of the liberal education system in Britain, coupled with a lack of understanding amongst the large majority of Britons today of the new settlers' *Faiths—Hinduism, Islam* and *Sikhism*—it is essential that we meet the challenge that our multi-religious society presents. Among practising families, *Hindu* children will not eat any kind of meat at school, *Sikh* children will not eat beef and *Muslim* children will not eat any non-ritually slaughtered meat and pork; this is a common enough phenomenon in multi-racial schools. Muslim children have shown a reluctance to take off their clothes for gymnastics and to participate in mixed bathing, Sikh children will not take off turbans even in the classroom. This is part of their religious practices, which along with a host of others in situations in and out of school, the three contributors have discussed taking care, at the same time, to establish what is purely religious, hence obligatory, and what is socio-cultural, hence subject to innovations. However unpalatable their explanations may be to the orthodox adherents the authors have embarked upon their venture to demonstrate that the *Faiths* do meet the criticism with rationale if need be. The practice of the *Hindu* caste system, which is rapidly disappearing, for example, is incomprehensible to an average Westerner who may take it as a purely religious division rather than based on race character-traits, professional pursuits, social abnormalities and physique of different races in the vast sub-Continent.

The history and synthesis in the *Hindu* society through the ages of Indus-Gangetic civilisation, different *Muslim* empires, the British kingdom and the *Hindu* and *Sikh* rules and the way *Hinduism* evolved through cultural patterns *vis-à-vis* the dogmatic preaching of the founders of *Islam* and *Sikhism* have been discussed briefly. There is an apt reference for the reader who may be interested in forecasting the future growth of these *Faiths* in the light of the genesis of the *Muslim* and *Sikh* communities living amidst the singular *Hindu* community in India centuries ago. The authors aim here not at proselytising but at preaching tolerance and understanding.

The British have dealt with these religious communities in all aspects of life during their rule in the sub-Continent. There are a host of lessons for the race relations worker in Britain to learn from this period of Indian history. The British administration during the two World Wars marshalled the Indian *Gurkhas, Muslims* and *Sikhs* against Germany who was preoccupied with greed to rule the world. It meant that *Sikhs* could wear turbans instead of helmets in meeting flying bullets on the battlefields, *Muslims* prayed without any let or hindrance and they all had food of their own specification made available to them.

Britain has long ceased to rule India, and the *Faiths* continue. The British people are gradually learning that, like the Christian Sabbath the day of rest, certain days have special significance for people of other religions, Sunday to a *Christian,* Saturday to a *Jew* and Friday to a *Muslim* bear implications for the adherents of the respective faiths. The *Muslim* believes that the Prophet *Adam* (peace be on him) was created, granted admission to Heaven, sinned, was driven out and sent to Earth and died; all these events having taken place on Friday which will also be the *Day of Judgement* and *Resurrection*. The fact that a number of children stay away from school and workers from jobs for Friday afternoon prayers is well-known to the non-*Muslim*.

There is a great deal to be known about the Festivals of Asian *Faiths*. Accordingly, a good deal of space has been devoted to these occurrences and their significance. Besides the descriptions of the rituals on these occasions, the essential characteristics of tolerance, trustworthiness, justice and fair-play, which are expected from these *Faiths,* have been referred to in the texts. The concepts of equality of the human race in terms of opportunity and the treatment, as believed and practised amongst the followers of the *Faiths* now and in the past, are vividly narrated. The honesty, for instance, of a fruit and vegetable vendor on the roadside in Indo-Pakistani cities and towns weighing his commodities in scales using stones equivalent to standard weights and his customers' trust beautifully depicts the moral values enshrined in the *Faiths*.

The study seeks to dispel widely misunderstood behaviour, in theory and practice, of the Asian communities in Britain. The status of womenfolk is one example, where even Asians are sometimes at a loss because of the complex nature of the issue. "In the laws of Islam on the subject of inheritance females are worth half and on matrimony only a fourth of the male" was the conclusion of a Turkish poet *Zia,* who influenced *Mustafa Kamal Ata-Turk* in his later reforms, and erroneously agitated over inequality of men and women in *Islam*. What the poet overlooked is that the *Muslim* family laws offer a woman, as a daughter, sister, wife and mother, more economic opportunities than a man. She is embraced and protected in the institution of marriage. Traditions are similar amongst the *Hindu* and *Sikh* communities.

We sincerely acknowledge the interest displayed by the Commission for Racial Equality in the *Faiths* and their help in making this publication possible. This publication follows naturally from *East Comes West*, last published by the former Community Relations Commission in conjunction with the Yorkshire Committee for Community Relations in 1973.

Muhammad Iqbal
The Polytechnic
Queensgate
Huddersfield HD1 3DH

HINDUISM

by Dharam Kumar Vohra

India is a landscape of religious life, a universe in itself, or one may say a constellation of faiths clustered together. As a religion the term Hinduism stands for Sanatan Dharama – the Primeval or the Eternal Religion. The faith is primeval because 'it reaches back to an age in history that can only be dimly surmised.' It is eternal in the sense that its fundamental ideas have asserted themselves in the successive movements of Jainism, Buddhism, Vaishanavism, Sikhism and numerous old and new creeds. The paramount concepts of Hindu faith are the *guardian ideas* of all the Indian religions in every sense of the phrase.

It is also known as Vedic Dharama or the Religion of the Vedas because the Vedic hymns provide us with the earliest picture of man's spiritual adventure into the realms of the Mysterious Unknown. Here we see the earliest spiritual consciousness which is diffused among all the latter movements of religious thought of India.

The Indus Valley Civilisation

Somewhere around 2500-2000 BC the Aryans came to the Indian sub-Continent through Persia and the high passes of Asia Minor, so giving the modern countries of Pakistan and India a common historical background of at least 45 centuries of recorded history.

These wandering resilient people who spread from the central steppes of Eastern Europe, and left their racial memory in the minds of many white Europeans up to the Arctic circle of Iceland and Sweden, have, in a sense made the white-skinned Europeans the blood brothers of the brown or darker-skinned races of the sub-Continent of India. In fact we have a common ancestry in our common progenitors, the Indo-Aryan progenitors.

But the Aryans, for so long held as the creators of Indian civilisation, are not now regarded as such. Recent excavations of the Indus Valley civilisation by such well-known TV personalities as Sir Mortimer Wheeler have begun to discover, at a deeper level of digging, certain terracotta figurines and medallions (one in Yogic Asna or posture) which indicate that the strongly ascetic tradition which we all recognise as characteristic of Indian thought was long-established before the Aryans spread into India.

In conquering, settling and finally inter-marrying with the indigenous race of darker-skinned Dravidians who had established their own culture and traditions, the Aryans asserted themselves, so pushing the Dravidians further south into that downward-pointing triangle of India, and giving that part of the continent its own particular flavour. South Indians are on the whole darker-skinned, and have differing facial structure from the Northerners—many of whom are, except for their black hair, as pale and 'Aryan' as a pure Englishman, if there is such a person, considering the mixture of English racial stock. This goes for Pakistanis too, some of whom have blue eyes and fair hair – another indication of our linked ancestry.

The Aryans established a strong rural society based on their particularly delicate but productive breed of cattle which they had brought with them across all of Middle Asia . . . . . . said by some authorities to be the original reason for the cult of the sacred cow. Their cattle were precious commodities in an essentially agricultural society, as the cow was also sacred to the early Egyptians. The Aryans also brought with them a marked disposition for pondering upon the awe-inspiring nature of the universe and the enormity of its comprehensiveness. These ideas were carried by memory in the thousands of verses of poetic philosophy which eventually were written down a thousand years later or more in the books known as the four Vedas – Rig, Yajar, Sām and the Atherva.

The earliest approach
There is no indication of idol worship in the Vedic hymns. They reverenced nature without temples but with pantheistic vision. Nature was to them fully animated and symbolised by the God of Fire – Agni, with three forms – terrestrial as fire; atmospheric as lightning; and celestial as the sun.

Heaven and earth – 'Akāsh' and 'Dharti' – are also symbolic of vastness and brightness and their union represents the earliest Vedic conception of creation based on an indissoluble connection between these two worlds – celestial and terrestrial. Here again the basic principle of the scientific inter-linking of Ether (Akāsh) and Matter (Dharti) is already significantly acknowledged by these thinkers, long before the modern academic study of physics propounded the same view. Ushā—Dawn is generally described in metaphorical language, giving insight into the cosmic harmony of man and nature in optimistic and life affirming attitudes (accidentally these Vedic names are still used as personal names for modern Indian women).

Indra, the prominent divinity, and atmospheric god, is often identified with thunder, and the wielding of his weapon – Vajra – as thunderbolt. This is the destroyer of demons, dread winds and darkness.

Surya, the Sun god, not only illuminates, but warms also, and sets life into motion with its energy. It, too, is the destroyer of darkness and ignorance, providing active life to the being. Chandra, the Moon, also had a significant godly role at night but the sun is the best image of the divine used by the Aryans, Iranians and others. They worshipped all the five elements of nature: Agni – fire, Vāyu – air, Jal – water, Dharti – earth, and Akāsh – ether or space. Even in the myths the sun god and the moon god were not shown without female companionship – Ushā, the dawn, and Sandhyā, the evening.

In the beginning the Aryans did not perceive any difference between body and spirit, but as the natural order of law, harmony and balance in the universe and in the forces of nature began to impinge on their intellect, these Hindu philosophers realised that independent natural forces would shatter the universe to pieces if unrelated to and uncontrolled by a single entity. The natural forces remained the object of worship but the concept of natural law behind them was given a new content and impetus. Anarchy was against the natural law of being. In their eyes the world now became a new ordered Cosmos. The tendency to see order in external nature, to unify the world and place it under the control of God can result in seeing Him somewhere in or beyond the space. But how can he control men? The only answer the Ayran found was that He controls from both inside and outside. Call Him Ishwara, Paramātmā or the Supreme Spirit, only He is the Highest controlling power, the source of light, both internal and external, and all the deities, therefore, submit to Him. He is the creator, the Supreme Spirit, Param Atmā i.e. the Greatest Soul (Atmā being the personal soul).

It is sometimes said that India is a land of religions. It has indeed many branches of a single religion i.e. Hinduism, and, therefore, many deities. Hence the charge of polytheism. The reason is that there has never been rigidity or final sanction of the Divine Law. Man's mind and intellect has never been given to any restricted thinking in any given order, because there has been no organised or institutional body such as church, nor theological creed to impose an attitude of rigid control upon the Hindu mind. Buddhism, Jainism and Sikhism all are restatements of old faith. None of them claims revelation of spiritual truth to the exclusion of other faiths. With an exception of a few religions such as Islam and Christianity all religions of India are but reform movements of Hinduism, part and parcel of the Indian way of life because the content of all of them is almost the same, with similarity of method in the ways of worship for the same ultimate purpose. They are the products of Indian soil and the Hindu mind.

What is called Hinduism in the strictest sense is based on the Vedas, also called the Shrutis (the word Shruti in Sanskrit meaning, 'what is heard'). The Vedas are sometimes claimed to have been heard by the sages in their forest retreats or Ashrams, and the truth in them said to have been revealed intuitively by 'knowing' just as the light of the sun is the direct means of our knowledge of form and colour. The Vedas are also called Shruti because their knowledge has been passed to the pupil by the preceptor through word of mouth long before it was recorded. The Vedas are, therefore, utterances of inspired seers known as Rishis claiming contact with transcendental truth.

The Vedas are the celebrated works which constitute the basis of Hindu

3

religion. The Rig Veda is the most ancient monument of Hinduism. This assemblage of the 1017 oldest hymns has been assigned to a period between 4000 and 2500 BC prior to the Aryans' settlement in India. The seers of "the Vedas were the first to burst in the sea of silence." Here we come across men seeking to know something greater than a day-to-day religion, and 'delving into the secret mystery of the Universe – the highest and the greatest truth'. Each of the four Vedas has two distinct parts – the Mantras the prayers and adorations often addressed to the elements of nature; the Brāhman Granths detailing ceremonies, and the appropriate chants for the given ceremonies, their explanations and the legends connected with them. The Brāhman Granths, not to be confused with the priestly class, are a part of the Aryan literature. There are three kinds of mantras, namely Rik, the verses in metre meant to be recited loudly, Yajus are in prose to be recited in low tone; the Samas which are in metre are intended for chanting. It is perhaps the Sāmas which are the ancestors of Indian classical music – Sangeet.

The Brahmana portion grows further in two parts, the Sutras i.e. the aphoristic rules, and the Upanishads. While the Brāhmanas, which are the liturgical books of the Aryan literature, represent the ritual portion, the Upanishads represent the knowledge portion. Tradition acknowledges one hundred and eight Upanishads but the principal Upanishads generally known are ten.

The Upanishads and the Essential Philosophy of Hinduism
In Sanskrit the word Upanishad approximates to the meaning in English – the nearest approach (to God), Upanish—sitting down near the preceptor to gain knowledge at his feet· that is to destroy ignorance by revealing knowledge of the supreme spirit.

Philosophically the great Upanishads wrangle with discourses of the most abstruse kind about the nature of Good and Evil, in man and the universe. It is from these questions and answers between guru and shishya or pupil that the recent Vedantic philosophy which has influenced the West has found its inspiration. Vedanta means 'the depth of the Vedas'.

One interesting thing to note is the anonymity of the Upanishadic thinkers—the Rishis or learned seers who first conceived these fundamental dialogues. This is so unlike the Greeks who put their name to their philosophical treatise, perhaps they were over conscious of mortality.

This emphasis on code and ritual bred its own reactions in the forest books or Aranyakas—and the Upanishads, circa 800 BC—the most elevated questioning of the whole fundamental nature of man and his place and meaning in the cosmic world beyond his reach, which came into being as the dialogues between the guru or the holy teacher and the pupil sitting at his feet.

These metaphysical concepts were at such an intellectual and spiritually

4

refined level that naturally enough religious thought had to be brought down into terms of every day life and concepts with which the ordinary villager could cope. There was, therefore, further development from pure metaphysics to a code of ethics and behaviour. So the Smritis (codes of law) and the epics of the Ramayana (9th century BC) and the Mahabharata (6th century BC) evolved.

The Rāmāyana

The Rāmāyana consists of 24,000 couplets. It is one of the most popular religious books of the Hindus. Written circa 900 BC the evidence of a single authorship and a poetic aim have given to the figure of Valmiki a definiteness and secured for him the title of Ādi Kavi—the Founder of Poetry. It is a work of a super-human consistency, composed with the peerless passion of a poet, prudence of a philosopher and the soothing sagacity of a sage.

The Rāmāyana is very different from the martial Epic of its successor. Here the values of bravery, truthfulness and especially loyalty are stressed in a somewhat didactic and practical manner.

The atmosphere of the Rāmāyana is tinged with lyricism and such an idealism that makes every character represent a type which each Hindu should attempt to attain. It tells the story of Rāma, the crown prince of Ayodhya, a Northern Kingdom in Uttar Pradesh, who is, at the same time, the ideal husband of Sita; the ideal brother of Lakshmana; the ideal son of the King of Ayodhya; the ideal warrior; the ideal friend and the ideal devotee. In Indian schools which include the Christian convent schools, Indian children of all faiths are taught to revere Rāma as the essence of what a man should try to be, and Sita as the ideal of womanhood, chaste, modest and all obedient to her husband. Even the birds, animals and plant life seem to exude a poetic state of optimistic joy and reverence, and are 'alive' to the 'dharma' the eternal order of right living.

The unjust exile of Rama; the capture of Sita by the demon-king Rāvana (regarded by some Indians as more a mixture of a fallen angel rather than an outrightly wicked villain); the rescue of Sita by an army of monkeys headed by the inventive Hanumān, the Monkey God (the reason for the sacred nature of India's vast monkey population) have all inspired countless subsidiary tales and dramas and dance poems as the Mahābhārata has done.

At a more subtle level of influence, the Rāmāyana has become a holy book to the Hindu. Rāma, because of the nature of his incarnation, is also a God to whom Hindus bow down in reverence and upon whom they call when the bodies are taken down for cremation.

'Rām naam satya hai' is the cry,
'The name of Rām is the truth'.

As a symbol of the divine forces of goodness, the whole story of his eventual reunion with Sita spells out the conflict between good and evil, and the eventual overcoming of the latter. This is enacted out year by year over the centuries in the village kathā, the dramas or Ramlilas, in the colourful and dramatic Hindu festival of Dussehra which takes place some time in September/October, and in the folk songs of the itinerant musicians and holy men. It is not known by formal scripture lesson but by the immediacy of a living culture which is very much in the air of India.

Mahābhārata

The historical development and enlargement of the Mahābhārata (the longest single poem in the world, consisting of 200,000 verses, (seven times the length of the two Greek epics combined) took well over a thousand years to achieve its present form—from about 900 BC when a historical battle was fought at Kurukshetra in the Punjab up to about AD 500 when it was finally completed.

The enduring story of the battle between cousins, the Pāndavas and the Kauravas; the romantic story of Damyanti, the beautiful princess and Nala, her Prince Charming; the lyrical love story of Shakuntala (as famous in India as Hamlet in Britain)—these have all served as the roof themes for infinite variations in Indian literature right up to the present age. They have also influenced and been depicted in sculptural form upon the temple walls, in the exquisite miniature paintings by Muslim artists in the Moghul period and in the evocative poetry both of pure literature and love songs, in classical dance forms of Bharat Natyam and the stylised mime-dance of Kathakali and drama.

The Bhagvad Gitā

What the Bible is to Christianity, the Gitā is to Hinduism. Even today in Britain, in the quietude of Hindu homes, the Gitā is read aloud to the children by their mothers. It is recited in the ceremonies and read at the funeral pyres at cremation. Although the Mahabharata, which includes the Gitā, is in the form of an epic in the Greek manner, of a gigantic battle between warring cousins, the Pandavas and the Kauravas, the essential rich philosophy of Hinduism is taught by the god Krishna in the form of imagery concerning the battle within the spirit and emotion of mankind to Arjuna, the princely archer of the Pandvas whose name means 'that which is unbound.'

He speaks on the philosophy concerning a human being's duty in this world; the idea of renunciation: of selfless action dutifully undertaken without thought for the egotistical fruits of that action; of liberation beyond the confining framework of human flesh and bone into the realms of spirit and imagination where all beauty and oneness lies.

"Among the priceless teachings", says Annie Basant in the introductory passage of Bhagvad Gitā, "that may be found in the great Hindu poem of the

Mahabharata, there is none so rare and precious as the 'Bhagvad Gitā, or the Lord's Songs.' The eighteen discourses consisting of 697 verses fell "from the divine lips of Shri Krishna (one of the incarnations of Vishnu) before the battle commenced". Independent of the Mahabharata the Gitā has become a world classic on its own merit in the field of religion. The Gitā is a Yoga Darshana—a philosophy of Union. It is a work of profoundly exalted intellectual as much as spiritual of a sage who puts all the varying strands of Hindu metaphysics together.

"The Gitā", says J. W. Hauer, an exponent of German faith, "is a work of imperishable significance. The book gives profound insights that are valid for all the times and for all religious life; a classical presentation of one of the most significant phases of Indo-Germanic religious history. Here spirit is at work which belongs to our own spirit". According to Huxley, "The Bhagvad Gitā is perhaps the most systematic spiritual statement of the Perennial Philosophy". "Many regard it", says Dr. Radhakrishanan, "as metaphysics and ethics combined together: it is science of Reality and the art of Union with Reality". From the outer planes of the Kurukshetra we can easily pass into the inner battle-field of the struggling soul—Arjuna, the boundless spirit of man being guided by Shri Krishna, the Logos of the Soul. Here we see in the Gitā that God, the goal becomes God, the guide of an aspiring soul.

The Vedic seers formed the conception of a being who is the source of all powers and forces of nature 'from whom nature with its manifold creatures has emanated and by whom it is sustained and maintained, and that there is one fundamental Reality in which all duality ceases'. This Reality is both imminent in the world and transcendent. They do not raise any question to rationalize their conceptions of the Ultimate. The Upanishads come up with some ground to assert the faith of the Vedas from their personal experience. The most delicate and intricate spiritual experiences and assertions are communicated through parables and dialogues. In this way they have laid the foundation of all later Hindu philosophy and its six major schools of which Sāmkhya of Sage Kapila is the earliest and Yoga of Sage Patanjali is most celebrated. In fact the Sākhya and Yoga in their various forms have most profoundly influenced Hindu culture and religion in their varied aspects, and this is through the Bhagvad Gitā that all diversities and apparently different approaches to the same end are unified. The paths are different! One chooses to tread the road one knows best and finds comfortable. All that matters is the goal. The Gitā has become a pocket-shrine of every Hindu no matter how he approaches the Divine.

The Purānas
History is said to be a continuous methodical record of important or public events especially those of the past. The Purāna means 'old or ancient'. There

are 18 chief Purānas which give to the Hindu 'a legendary history of prominent clans such as the Solar clan or dynasty of Rama Chandra of the Rāmāyana, and the Lunar dynasty of Krishna of the Gitā. The extensive Puranic literature portrays in the form of legends those ideals which the sagacious ancestry duly bequeathed to the later generations. The governing principles and fundamentals of good conduct are not handed to Hindus by the priest but by mothers through bedtime stories from the Purānas from early childhood.

Wisdom of the Old
Hinduism can claim no founder, no central authority like the Church, no institutional organisation, no creed. It does in fact far transcend the area of religious involvement as we know it in the West. Hinduism is a mixture of a living philosophy of the most profound kind, a temple ritual which has confused the foreigner; ancient traditions of social customs which have the strength of at least four thousand years development behind them, and recently sweeping movements of social reform which now find a focus in the saintly scholar Vinobhā Bhāve working at the humble village level, who walked the face of India with nothing but a typewriter to his name.

India's religious traditions are legion but those founded on the Vedas are considered to be the highest because they have stood the storm of history and come through the tests of time, whereas other comparatively new and modern ones have vanished.

It may come as a surprise to the Westerner to be told that the world's oldest surviving faith is, in its concepts, remarkably modern. The hymns of the Vedas emerging around 2500-2000 BC had already conceived of the truths about the universe which the people in the West are only now coming to accept as scientific truths. Hindu cosmology has always worked on an immense astronomical scale the same as that now opening to the West through radio astronomy.

The early Aryan had already arrived at these concepts by another route, that of spiritual and mystical intuition. There is at least a 4500 years reservoir of thought and knowledge about man and his relationship with the universe in the Hindu study of astrology, astronomy, psychology, mathematics and metaphysics.

The Hindu Epics are full of references and stories about journeys made to the Chandra Lok (the world of the moon) and Surya Lok (the world of the sun) and many other planets. There are references to 'Amogh-shakti'—in Sanskrit, an uninterceptible rocket which must hit its target—in the Mahabharata. The concept of the atom, and the highly developed harnessing of mind and spirit and emotion to a disciplined framework of Yoga, was already 4000 years in advance of the modern psychosomatic medical discoveries. For this reason nothing is really new to a Hindu. He is an adaptive person who finds the new in the old and the ancient in the supposedly new.

The Upanishadic philosophers had also discussed creative energy in the terms of modern biology—that is an evenly balanced relation of male and female principles. These abstract ideas later appear on the mythological scene in the form of complementary deities such as Siva and Shakti, Vishnu and Lakshmi, Rāma and Sita, and Krishna and Rhādā—which are only a few to be mentioned and worshipped every day by the Hindu peasant and priest alike.

This probably accounts for the inherent quality of the gods and goddesses in the Hindu Pantheon, and also for the venerable place the Hindu woman so persistently finds in home and Indian society. In fact, because of this philosophic idea founded upon biological principles, there has always been an acceptance of equivalence of the male and female authority which only during periods of alien invasions (such as Muslim attacks from the Near East and the European Raj) became circumscribed by the need to protect women from abduction and the perils of free movement in society.

The other scriptures after the Vedas represent interpretations and codifications of Vedic truth and are, therefore, called Smitris i.e. human traditions retained generation by generation in the form of hearing from one to the other, or recorded experience from traditions. The Hindu may also believe that his personal deity to whom he worships, and whose image (often made of bronze carving) resides in his house, reveals a rare facet of the Divine in some still more recent experiences.

The Hindu sees in the whole development of Hinduism the emphasis of different aspects of the Vedas, as a gradually deeper and more complete perception of the truth which was in the Vedas all the time, but which becomes clearer with the growth of man's perception over the centuries. All the main schools of philosophy which exist within Hinduism, therefore, claim Vedic authority, a claim which later Hindus have accepted in the belief that all were complementary of the one Truth, and later movements are just a continuation and expansion of the earlier faith. Even Buddhism which is sometimes considered independent of Hinduism has not rejected the authority of the Vedas.

The Trinity of Godhead

What is distinct in modern Hinduism, is that sometimes Brahma or God is worshipped as Nirguna—without quality or description, and sometimes as Saguna—with quality. The latter implies the worship of a personal god seen in idol, picture or image of an object or incarnation. Although there is no watertight compartment in this case, the main personal gods are a trinity of Brahmā, Vishnu and Shiva. Philosophically these are three symbolic expressions of the attributes of the Divine. Brahmā is the creator; Vishnu, the preserver and sustainer of universe, and Shiva, the source of creative energy and its ultimate destruction for the sake of further reconstruction of virtue. In none of these is there idol worship—the content behind the image is the primary concern.

Though it will be hard to find one who follows the purely Vedic traditions, there are those who at least try to do so, and are known as the Ārya Smājists, the society of the Aryans. Any kind of picture of God or an idol to worship is generally against their principle. They believe in God without quality or form, Brahma as the impersonal abstract.

The Sagunists or the believers of God in a form or with quality strictly adhere to Brahmā, Vishnu, Shiva, their consorts and their progeny who gave rise to the expanding world of the Hindu Pantheon of deities.

Brahmā

Brahmā as a manifestation of the abstract idea of divinity is not much evidently worshipped although known to every Hindu, and mentioned in every religious ceremony. Brahmā is the symbolic expression of Brahm which means 'that which moves everywhere, a force which moves in everything, the source of expansion of the universe'.

Shiva

God in the form of Shiva is very popularly worshipped. Shiva has an infinite number of attributes and powers; is free from all taints and defects; Lord of the whole material and spiritual universe. He is called Bhāve because he exists everywhere and at all times. He is Sarve because he destroys everything; Pashupati because he is the Lord of physicality in the sense of animal passion; Rudra because he removes the sorrows of the world; Shiva because he is free from all taints and he is called Kāla which means 'Time'. He is supremely auspicious. He is the cause of creation, maintenance and dissolution of the world, and by his grace cause of the liberation of souls through the cessation of their bondage to the process of rebirth. He is the enjoyer of his own infinite bliss.

In the most famous bronze image of Shiva, to be seen in the Victoria and Albert Museum in London, the conception of Shiva is again astonishingly modern. Shiva is Nata Rāja, the God of Dance ringed with fire, the symbol of his aspect of Destroyer of the universe. This imagery of Godhead holds within his dancing frame the symbolism of life sparkling from inert matter into the energy of motion, like particles in the gases of outer space, only to die away again in the final flames of destruction to be followed by the same cyclical process of rebirth in the sparking off of conscious energy. Philosophy and science meet within the ring of fire. He is formless prior to the creation and withdraws all his powers within himself; he assumes shape or form when he expands these powers and is about to create the world. He is not different from the creation as the snake is not different from its coils; the unity is there like the moon and its beams. He is the efficient and material cause of the world.

Through his Shakti (female energy) he creates the world. The beat of his 'Dumru' (a drum shaped like an hour glass) sets the universe to a dancing life, and the rhythm is the expression of the control of time, and a symbol of the law of continual movement and flux in the universe into which Shiva pours forth his energy in dancing.

Vishnu
God in the form of Vishnu is said to be the source, the transcedent God of the created worlds. In one of the famous scriptures depicting Vishnu, He lies upon the waters of life which feed creation (again this could be linked to an early symbolic interpretation of the process of DNA, the nucleic acid which sustains all life) and the elementary material aspect, the first tangible emanation of the Divine, which though beyond form, yet evolves and comprehends all forms. In sculptural representation these are symbolised in the coils of the huge serpent whose dwelling is the cosmic abyss, and whose name is 'Ananta', the Endless. Images breathe personified philosophy.

For this reason, perhaps, snakes are held sacred in India and not regarded with the evil connotations as in the West. In South India, in the groves and corners of gardens on the Malabar Coast, there is often a shrine to the Naga or snake, and milk is placed for serpents' replenishment.

God as Vishnu reclines on his immeasurable body from which our temporal existences spring. Ananta supports in his expanded hood both terrestrial and celestial spheres. He is the everliving cosmic ocean which is perpetually transforming its movements and colours. Vishnu is the personified 'Purusha' of the Vedas, the primeval living spirit, the Eternal man who becomes incarnate in a portion of his essence to deliver mankind from evil, and to establish the value of virtuous life . . . . . Dharama.

Avtār—Incarnation
The idea of Vishnu as God developed into numeruous forms of incarnations or the Avtārs chiefly Rama and Krishna, and many others believed to be 10, sometimes 24. The theory of avatārs or extremely holy spirits born in human form, assumes divine concern for human endeavour. God is the light in us. Our part is to open our being to this emanation. When the light in us comes to possess our being we speak of birth of God within us. The incarnation is not a special event but a continuous process of expression of the divine in His drama.

The Avtārs appear not only to put down evil but also to teach mankind and establish the codes of duty which becomes dissipated in the course of time and ossified by social customs.

11

Dharam samsthāpanārthāye sambhavāmi yugeh yugeh' says
Krishna in the Gitā.
'I come from age to age to re-establish codes of duties as they
are needed'.

Krishna

Great souls appear for the well-being and spiritual enlightenment of mankind to tell us to remould our lives. The Divine forces are always prepared to help us provided we are prepared to call on them.

'Bhaktānām anukamparthanam devo vigrahvān bhavet' says
the Brahma Sutra. 'Out of compassion for the devotees the
Supreme assumes a human form.'

In the Hindu view such great souls have come to all mankind. Buddha, Christ and Muhammad are such ones. The Lord Krishna teaching the Yoga of englightenment in the Bhagvad Gita is the God of redemption of mankind, a manifestation of Love, Devotion, Duty and Action.

In a way the unfamiliar mind sees in Hinduism a sort of image worship but the way it is taken and adopted in the Hindu life is really worship of the symbol of the Divine. It is an aid to worship. The symbol is not the image. Slowly—the Hindu reasons, we get beyond the symbol to the object symbolised until we reach the ultimate goal. We gain rewards great or small according to our aims and object. Image worship is a means to that realisation. When we gain our ends, the means fall away. Lamps are useful so long as we live in darkness. When the sun rises, they cease to be of any help. When the Ultimate Reality floods the spirit of man 'the earth is crammed with heaven, and every common bush afire with God'. Santayana was right to emphasise, that 'the in-dwelling ideal lends all the gods their divinity'.

Obviously spiritual knowledge and refinement is meant for the whole of mankind and not only for the philosophers or the pundits. Philosophy has got to be brought down to earth to the simple house-holder who has no dictates to follow. Man in the street has no time for abstract thoughts although there is neither rigid injunction to obey nor a dogma to follow. The Hindu has learnt since his childhood the purpose of life. The ideals of bedtime stories vibrate in his spirit all through the life. The ideals are cherished and worshipped.

Daily Worship

Worship is obeisance, an expression of total submission to God. Although there are temples all over the Hindu world, there is no specific time, place or way of worship. It can be conducted at any place, time and in any manner one wishes. In day to day simple life, from the time an orthodox Hindu wakes in the morning (at a very early hour 4 or 5 am) a bath must first be taken, or a good bodily wash. Cleansing the body is essential before prayers can be said. The act of washing in fact becomes time enough in which to meditate upon the process of prayers.

In such a warm climate the Hindu, if he can, goes either to a holy tank (pond) or river and immerses himself so that direct contact with natural elements is made. If a woman, she goes in sari and all, and skilfully unwinds into another dry sari on coming out of the water. A few personal prayers or mantras are said accordingly to family traditions or as taught by the personel guru while sprinkling water through the fingers in worship to the rising sun—symbol of the giver of life. In such a way humbleness attitude is inculcated of being part of the natural process of creation rather than being an arrogant man set above nature.

After the prayer a Hindu will take up his brass pitcher and fill it with water, then cast its contents away facing the sun. He can equally do this at the well or in the temple, and throw it over the Shiva lingam or phallic symbol of the generative processes of life creation. This black stone lingam is placed in the temple or under the spreading shade of the great peepul trees where the oxygen is most fresh in the early morning air.

The theory behind this simple ceremony is that of shramadān— the charity of labour in the deeper sense of charity rather than for any expected reward. A Westerner seeing this may wonder why on earth the worshipper is taking up water only to throw it away again. Why so foolish? The Hindu sees this as a dedication, involving his labour without looking for any reward. Each day this becomes a constant reminder of yet another discipline to the ultimate creative process of life which will be carried subconsciously throughout his future life.

Only now can the worshipper take food. Even then a tiny portion is set aside on his thal or plate before commencing his own meal, again to remind him of charity.

If he can afford it, not being of the class that has to go straight out to till the fields in the cool of the early morning before the heat reaches 115°, he goes also to the temple, and is given a prasād by the pandit or priest. Prasād is a word meaning kindness or beneficence and is symbolised by a sweetmeat made from milk, ghee and sugar placed in a peepul leaf plate, taken in cupped hands. Even rice or a petal of a flower or a jasmin garland (never to be smelled as this would pollute it) may be given as a token of God's benevolence in the house of God. Or the priest will place a sandalwood mark—the tikā—upon the forehead, or three stripes for Shiva or a 'U' mark for Vishnu. The three stripes are parallel. The small red spot is not to be confused with 'Bindi', the decorative red spot worn by the Hindu and Sikh women on their foreheads.

This kind of worship can be repeated at any time of the day or night, for that matter as the temple is open all the time and one is free to enter at any time. Shoes must be left always out of the door of the shrine. Each family follows its own form of worship from long force of tradition.

There are certain times when gods and goddesses are 'woken up' like the rest of human beings, given baths and are fed coconut-milk, saffron and rice. These are accompanied by ringing bells and incense, and the temple is flooded with classical music—and in the old days, the dedicatory temple dance of India.

A foreigner travelling from Cape Comorin to the Himalayas will meet the Indians almost of different notions. A Madrasai may only be able to speak to a Punjabi in English to be understood. A Hindu from Rajasthān is very different racially from a Keralā or a Bengāli Hindu—but they are all bound by common background and basic conceptions of faith. Even their rituals, traditions and family customs may be radically different but without the slightest hesitation they will all understand the basic terms and important expressions of Hindu view and way of life. This is what unites them and makes them one people.

Purpose of life

Everything that lives, aims at a specific perfection of its own nature. The sub-human species work according to pre-determined pattern but man due to his creative urge has to achieve fulfilment by his effort and will. Man is not completely a victim of circumstances. He can say 'No' to life, and he can reject one kind of satisfaction for that of a higher kind. He can impose discipline on his own nature and check the drive of desire. He can create a new nature in which the different elements of his being are being harmonised. To the Hindu there is a strain in human life which impels one to introduce peace and order into the swarm of impulses, emotions and notions which are basically incongruous to the harmony of our own souls. To bring harmony in this field is a job which will take more than a life time. But humanity has an ache for perfection and wholeness, and an anguish for beatitude. Man's quest for perfection consists in organising things of body, mind and soul into a unity to attain the kingdom of heaven. So long as our natures are not integrated, our actions are confused and contradictory. In an integrated man thought, speech and action are of one piece. Yoga aims at integration of all parts of a human being into a perfected whole aiming at the union with the Divine, the Infinite whatever one chooses to call the Ultimate Reality behind the manifest universe.

Yoga

The Sanskrit word 'yog' has the same connotation as the English word 'yoke'—meaning 'togetherness' or binding together. The Yoga philosophy has come down to us from sage Patanjali circa 300 BC.

14

In the Western mind yoga is associated with body-twisting gymnastic exercises. The Hindu concept is very different indeed, seeing these specific, scientifically worked out postures as only a means to a much more comprehensive end. Through an efficiently run bodily system and properly concentrated breathing the mind can be so directed that the body is finally forgotten.

To the Hindu philosophers the theory that 'mind is matter' was not something to talk about theoretically in philosophical times, but concept upon which to act. Mind is not physical matter but subtle matter—we become what we think. This is why prayer and meditation still have such an emphatic hold even upon seemingly agnostic modern Indians. There can be no atheist in the Hindu view. No matter how much we deny God, we are God by the very nature of our creation.

The Eight Stages of Yoga
To achieve the end, being in the world but not of the world, eight progressively different stages of yoga evolve. These are:

1 *Yam*   (the curbing of instincts)
2 *Niyam*   (self restraints)
3 *Asana*   (yogic postures)
4 *Prānāyām*   (breath culture)
5 *Pratyāhāra*   (withdrawal of sense objects from their objects)
6 *Dhāranā*   (steadying the mind)
7 *Dhayān*   (yogic meditation)
8 *Samādhi*   (total yogic abstraction)

According to Krishna in the Gitā the purpose of yoga is to attain 'unwavering' firmness by which one restrains the activity of mind—'manah'; of the life-breath i.e. prāna; and of sense organs; the firmness which is pure, so essential to direct the mind, the body to the inner sources of energy or soul in a mystical and divine sense.

The resources are there within each human being but for the asking, and with right knowledge. Again a guru is necessary because the evolution of the soul is extremely delicate matter, and the processes of yoga so demanding as to be extremely dangerous to the uninitiated.

The yoga aims at the complete liberation from the claims of self—that is forgetfulness of self to become one with the Universe and its Maker. No doubt the way of yoga is not easy for all but there are other ways open.

The Governing Beliefs
For all schools of Indian religion and philosophy man is a wayfarer—Margika—from the outward world to inward reality—i.e. the

ultimate truth. During this journeying, man yearns for liberation—Mukti or Moksha—a liberation from the prison-house of human ignorance which is the cause of revolving cycle of birth, old age, death and rebirth. The Hindu striving, therefore, has been 'concentrated upon release from an existence governed by the law of cause and effect'. Moksha or liberation is the goal of life of the Hindu, the Sikh, the Jain and the Buddhist. Ignorance gives birth to illusion—Māya—leading to false judgement, wrong decisions hence unjust deed or evil action-bad karma. The Reality is not the tangible world we see around us in material terms but the illusive inner core of our beings (closer to the concept of spirit in the true Christian sense). God is within each of us in the very fact that we exist. The scientific process of creativity is God. Divinity is us. The Upanishads say: *tat twam asi—thou art that.*

The philosophical books are full of discourses on individual *atma* or soul in relation of the measureless Reality or great Soul—Param Atmā, otherwise called perfection or the Impersonal Absolute of which all of us are but minute parts, individual molecules enmeshed in an immense living whole.

Māyā

Māyā is a human ignorance, or knowledge without the rightful corollary of wisdom (an entirely different thing). For this the importance of the Guru, the guide, a competent teacher has been considered so important in all branches of life in Hinduism, Sikhism and others like Jainism and Buddhism that sometimes the Guru is placed as high as Godhead itself.

Karma in accordance with Dharma is a means through which liberation or Mukti is achieved. Dharma determines the course of Karma. Right knowledge, therefore, is necessary to tear away the curtains of illusion known as Māyā.

Karma—The way of Action

At all levels Hinduism is concerned in a continuing dialogue between the forces of Good and Evil, right and wrong. The world is a world of action—Karma which according to the Vedas is Duty—*Dharma*. A misconception held by westerners is that Hinduism is other-worldly. The law of Karma tells us in fact that as in the physical world, in the mental and moral world also there is law, which it is the duty of every man to follow. Karma is not a theory of fatalism. It is a supreme, inescapable law of cause and effect in spiritual as well as material development. Every act has its effect on personality whether the act be in thought, word or deed. This is universal law which must be followed by man otherwise the cancer of chaos sets in, as it happens in the realms of nature her immutable laws are broken and the cells explode into disorder.

Duty demands action—Dharma through Karma. It is a meritorious deed—Karma which sustains and supports the Universe. The creation of the world is due to Action—God had to act for it. Human action, therefore, is necessary, and according to its virtue, human action can transform the nature of the universe. Past Karma has determined the present nature of the world; the present Karma can shape the future of it.

'Karmamayam jagat' said the Aryan: 'World is an action'.
'Lokoyam Karambandhna', says Krishna in the Gitā: 'The world is bound by action'.

No action is ever lost. It may not produce immediate effect; it may remain in latent form until proper occasion for frutification comes. It becomes a potential energy. This is a highly activistic faith, and its doctrine is not merely fatalism. Our acts determine our character which in turn determines our acts. This emphasises the importance of conduct. It lays a heavy responsibility on each individual Hindu to strive towards his own salvation from his own inner 'call' towards good, the yearning for it, rather than because of outward admonishments arising from an external dogma, theology or a commandment saying THOU SHALT or THOU SHALT NOT.

The law of Karma is simply the organic nature of life where each successive phase grows inevitably from what has gone before, and where humanity, and therefore each individual as part of a gigantic whole, is subject to universal laws which hold everything in right balance. It intensifies our sense of tremendous importance of every decision we make for the right or wrong. This has not been made clear enough to the Western world. It has in fact nothing in common with predestination as is commonly supposed. It is the inescapable logic of the universe and presupposes the necessity of personal discipline, an inner authority, which impels us to obey the order of things.

Karma and Moksha or Mukti
Salvation or Moksha is not a gift of capricious gods but is to be won by earnest seeking. 'The moral law is fundamental to the whole cosmic drama.'' Man is the sole master of his own fate. Hindu religion does not believe in the mechanical view that the soul dies with the body. On the contrary it is firmly believed that "soul may not be fit for eternal life and goes from life to life until it is fit for eternal freedom—"the goal of human evolution". No doubt the body dies but the soul, the spark of the divine, has a continuous existence.

The Hindu believes that he will be rewarded for the good deeds during the cycle of rebirths in the near future. His meritorious acts will quicken the process of salvation. This is why even the temple level of Hinduism has remained so entrenched and important. Bad deeds, however, will retard this process. One bad act will put him in the yoke of a thousand more births and rebirths, a long and infinitely tiring process, and thus delay the union of this ātmā with God.

Besides, says the Hindu, you cannot escape the effect of cause. You must be rewarded for the good deed and punished for the bad Karma, the evil side of your active life, mental, physical or whatever you might call it. It is because of the ultimate logic of this system of thought, and the justice of it, that the doctrine of reincarnation has such a strong hold on the Hindu mind. There is no escape from the evil and the punishment due for it in this life or the next life beyond this one.

There is always certainty of the reward for good deeds and a good heart now and hereafter. This is why Hindu literature is full of hope without the slightest sense of tragedy until foreign influence through European literature, with its pessimistic strain, appeared in India and began to influence Indian thought (although indirectly). The sense of inescapable sin born as original sin within the West, so tarnishing one from birth even in the concept of sex, and also giving frailty to life is wholly foreign to the Hindu view of life.

According to this doctrine of reincarnation it takes thousands of rebirths (the layman knows this as 'chorāsi Lākh', 84 lākhs being the equivalent of 8,400,000) to enable the individual ego, *ātma* or soul to burn away the dross of evil, and gradually realize that higher state of awareness in future lives until the final absorption in the *Brahm* is attained.

'Why don't you believe in the evolution of soul in the same way as you believe in evolution, in a biological sense, of material life?'' is what a Hindu asks.

One life is too short to perfect the individual Atmā. After all how many aeons in the process of evolution it has taken to perfect man biologically from the ape! Man seems still lacking in too much in the search for spiritual perfection. Yet the Hindu reasons that despite our wayward natures the knowledge is unconsciously there that we must inevitably move towards goodness once we know how to harness these subconscious urges as, slowly our ignorance, in terms of the subtle body of spirit, is stripped away like the layers of an onion. When the price for wrong acts has been duly paid, and we have had time enough to till the ground and to nourish it, sowing the seeds in many lives, the time matures for the harvest to be reaped in its own patiently awaited time. It is this reason that gives the Hindu mind its tranquillity of spirit in a slow, unhurried way which many westerners misunderstand as a lack of urgency. Life to the Hindu, however, has no clearly defined horizon at its far edge; it has stretched too far back, and stretches too far away into the future. Immortality is life, in the past, here and now, and in the future. Sometimes at funerals in India the draped body is taken for cremation, accompanied by a band of male relatives singing with rejoicing at a long life lived rightfully. Death is not always an occasion for wails, weeping and mourning.

Dharma

The concept of Dharma is as important and popular among the Hindus, Buddhists, Jains, Sikhs and many others as that of Karma. In Sanskrit the word has many overtones meaning equally DUTY, QUALITY, NATURE, RIGHT, CONDUCT, MERIT, LAW, RELIGION, JUSTICE, and even REALITY. The word is derived from the Sanskrit root Dhr—to hold or maintain; that which upholds the essential nature of things. In this world everything has its essential nature such as burning is the essential nature of fire; inertia is the dharma of inanimate things. Similarly a human being has an essential nature that upholds his existence as something distinct from the rest of creation. Evidently the 'nature of becoming divine' marks out a human from all other animals.

While man walks along the road to eternity, and fulfilment of the highest goal, he is burdened with duties towards his fellow-beings, to pay what he owes to others, the family, the clan, the society, the country and the world which is not only the world of men and women but animals, birds and plants also. There is always a conflict of lower duties and the higher duties—the conflict between higher Dharma and the lower Dharma, where one has to sacrifice a lovely yet lower station of life for the sake of a higher ideal or Dharma. For a long period it has been considered both as meaning 'right' and 'good'. It has been accepted that whatever is good and right is Dharma.

The discrimination between right and wrong, the good and the bad, is not an easy task in the field of conduct when one has to take a life long decision, and this demands knowledge.

Gyān or the way of knowledge and Meditation

When knowledge is said to be the source or way to liberation, it does not mean some University degree or an intellectual equipment but spiritual wisdom. Man's intellect begins to weave webs around his ownself. Once he is tangled in, it is difficult to get out of the wire-net of logic. Yoga does still the outward activities and emotions, and helps in concentrating on the pure consciousness of the unknown but it needs a Guru—the guide, and when Gyāns attained the spirit is exalted to that degree that man feels to suffer for the entire humanity. Judgement of a clouded mind is unreliable.

There is a broad stream of spiritual knowledge in us. It requires us to grow to a higher level of being by an inner quickening and growth in our nature. The all-pervading Self abides in every heart. We have to strive to know the Real by means of inner consciousness. The vision of intellect becomes obscure, and it is dimmed by vice and weakness.

In moments of meditation we become self aware. With the ability to control our senses we do not loose the feel of the Eternal in the distractions of life; rather we acquire a trust that sustains us during the terrible catastrophies. We gain a loyalty to truth in the midst of passion and lure. Meditation is a medium but Gyān is Realization.

Bhakti or the way of Devotion

Bhakti Mārga or the way of devotion (Bhakti meaning intense loving devotion) has been accepted generally by every Hindu. It asserts that it is only through loving devotion that one can attain the unattainable. The way of devotion presupposes the recognition of a personal God (more in the sense of a loving God who cares for His children) who is omniscient, omnipresent, omnipotent, who confers His grace on the devotee, however lowly he may be, when he surrenders himself unreservedly to Him. The devotee finds supreme pleasure in God. Love of man and woman is commonly used to illustrate love of man for God. When the lovers are together, they are afraid of being separated; when they are not together, they have a painful desire for union, as is seen in the yearning desire of Radha for Krishna in his aspect as a playful Cupid, the blue-skinned God with his flute playing so effectively upon the heartstrings of the milkmaids who encircle him—a symbolic expression of playful relationship of humanity and God.

The followers of this path believe that liberation, realisation or perfection is possible only through devotion of the devotee's soul which itself is part of the Great Soul—Param Atmā. Even reason and intellect may be caught in the snares of Māyā (the illusion of objects surrounding us) whereas devotion moves on undeterred. Devotion means complete and exclusive absorption in God, and is indifferent to things opposed to Him. It is fruit in itself. God loves the meek, and devotion implies obedience to the will of the Supreme in all the actions of man. Choosing this path the Hindu is free to worship his personal God, male or female: to adore a representative image of the *Deva* which is usually kept in a niche, and decorated with flowers and saffron in the privacy of the home.

Hindu Pantheon of Deities

Out of this has arisen the huge Hindu pantheon of gods and goddesses, representing every kind of human yearning, even to the darkest side of man's nature in the bloodlust cult of the dark Goddess of destruction—Kāli Mātā. This multitude of aspirations has given rise to the idea that Hindus are polytheistic by nature, but scratch the surface of a Hindu and underneath he will be seen to resolve the multitude into a wholeness or unity—the one God. Singularity comes from the multifarious.

Each masculine symbol of Deity is equally balanced by a female symbol. In fact it is said by Indians that their Goddesses are more potent and powerful, and consciously acknowledged as such, than the male Gods. Shiva's consort Mātā Pārvati has in fact been given a variety of names according to her various

20

attributes and qualities. In fact she represents in general terms the two forms of feminine energy—one mild and protective (Umā, Jagatmātā, Gauri, Ambā and Pārvati), the other fierce and cataclysmic (Durgā, Kāli and Chandi). Although war-like in aspect, with ten arms flailing like a modern Picasso with ten instruments of destruction, Durgā is worshipped, especially by the Bengalis, as Mother who triumphs over evil. The Hindu does not forget that 'the hand which rocks the cradle, can **rock** the world!'

Gāyatri Mantra

Among the numerous religious hymns and chants the Gāyatri Mantra is as familiar and necessary to the Hindus as the Lord's Prayer to a Christian. It is chanted at all proper Hindu ceremonies, at birth, marriage and at formal blessings (for instance the opening of a new steel works or the inauguration of, say, the Radio Farm Forums on All India Radio) for an auspicious outcome for new undertakings.

'*Gāya*' means 'to sing', '*tri*' means 'three', '*mantra*' is a sung prayer or hymn. But *Gāyatri Mantra* is embedded in further symbolism to the Hindu.

It is also the hymn of Three meanings, repeated three times with an inbuilt triple rhythm in the Sanskrit words, containing a three-fold significance in metaphysical, philosophical and religious terms i.e. mind, speech and body.

The thought behind this all-important Mantra is that any act initiated by a human being is limited by these three. First the vow is given in the ceremony of the Godhead—Brahm: 'I submit to you to prepare me bodily. Secondly to give me the power to speak right thoughts, Thirdly to give me the power to think rightly for the sake of good'.

In Sanskrit the words are

Sukaram	—right action
Suvachan	—right speech
Suvichar	—right thought, implying the thought to every Hindu, framed as a prayer: *mansa vacha karmana*.

'I must be able to have right knowledge of the knowable
While making me a knower of the right
Because I want the knowledge for right action'.

The actual words of the Gāyatri Jāpam as it is called when repeated a number of times in invocation at any time of the day, especially early morning 'remembering' are these:

OM, Bhūr bhuvah svah
Tatsavitur varenyam
Bhargo devasy dhimahi
Dhiyo yo nah prachodayāt.

The full implication of the early Sanskrit are so dense linguistically—with overtones and undertones—that it is difficult to render a comprehensive translation into the English language. Sāvita (also spelled *Savtri, Savitu* and *Savitā* in English texts, but not to be confused with Savitri, a heroine of epic legend) the sun radiates light and consequently energy into the world. This is mental as well as physical energy. We know in scientific terms, geologically as well as astronomically that without the forces of energy, power, heat, the terrestrial planet on which we precariously exist, would atrophy into sterile and inert matter. Indeed in geological prediction we shall be eventually disintegrated. All creative life does depend upon the sun, and our delicate relationship with it.

Paraphrase of the Gāyatri Jāpam in English translation:

Aum,
Resplendent Savitā (Sun), inspiring us to reverence,
Let us dwell on the radiance
Of that guiding power
That charges us with light.

If we follow the age old credited method of exposition of these most ancient hymns in world knowledge, we find that every hymn has its own special deity (Devtā) imbued in it, so denoting its subject matter and evoking a mood, a 'rasa'—relish in music and other fine arts, as propounded by the Sage Bharata, the author of The Principles of Aesthetics, and the Manuals of Dramatic Art. The deity or the subject matter of this most revered hymn, Gāyatari, is Savitā which means the Progenitor, Creator or the sun.

The Creator can be conceived by all human beings both at the microcosmic and the macrocosmic levels. Equally the Creator works in creating at both levels separately and at one and the same time. Thus the meeting implied here are manifold, literally numberless, but in this mantra we are concerned with only two of them. One is the sun, the creator and illuminator of our solar system, including the earth and all life on it. The other one is the most important—the creating 'Being', the impersonal Absolute Brahm, the cause of all existence, including millions of stars larger than our sun. It is this Entity that is acknowledged in prayerful reverence by Hindus, dwelling upon it in meditative thought at the beginning of every day—a creative experience in itself, so often unremembered in the West where climate and architecture imprison the human being away from the ultimate forces of nature which shelter our fragile beings.

Remembering therefore with humility each morning these forces from which we draw our strength, the Hindu customarily initiates every hymn with the profoundly symbolic and fundamental sound: OM or AUM which means Turiya or pure consciousness, the attributeless Brahm.

Even by the mechanical process of intoning the Gāyatri a person is psychologically 'plugged in' to the electric current that radiates through and illumines the entire behaviour of man and his virtuous nature. Matter becomes motion, energising the inert. The world of physics is the world of Hindu metaphysics. The mantra holds the key to coming near to Godhead, and the very mouthing of its syllables is charged with a spiritual potency.

The Guru

No matter what goal of life, what ideal of profession one chooses one has to look for a guide. "A teacher affects eternity: he can never tell where his influence stops". The well known Indian saying sums up the importance of teacher to that degree that "there is no salvation without Guru".

'Gurur Brahmā, Gurur Vishnu, Gurur Devo Makeshvarah
Gurur sākshāt Pāra-Brahma, tasmai shree gurve namah'.

'I bow down therefore in homage to my Guru (preceptor) who not only represents the *Trimurti* (the three images of Trinity: Brahmā, Vishnu and Shiva) but also the whole universe (Pāra-Brahma) incarnate'.

This is the reason for due reverence still being given to the teacher in India. The Guru will choose the way he finds suitable and easy for the disciple or shishya according to his intellectual and spiritual capacity. How gratifying to learn from the British school teachers that 'Hindu children are very obedient'.

The goal is the same—liberation of the individual soul from the imprisoning sense of Māyā, and the merging of the soul into the Great Spirit—Param Atmā, the Brahm. This is the highest duty of man to lift the human soul to that standard where it is absorbed into the real life, where union with Godhead is achieved. This has led the Hindu to a very alive and constant concern with the investigating the true nature of Reality in his personal thinking and with a detached sense of illusion where the world around him is concerned.

Faith is a very personal individual discipline for the Hindu and cannot be dogmatised over by religious bodies. Each person's salvation is his own concern and a matter for his own searching, with power and devotion. This may explain why, in general, the Indian accepts more passively the upheavals of life rather than turning to the rebellious attitudes characteristic of the West. The restless ferment, change for change's sake, is not the concern of the Hindu. The searching is constantly into personality, into the inner reality. It may also account for his acceptability of new conditions and environments as he is only beholden to his own moral conscience. An Indian enjoys perhaps the widest ranging intellectual liberty of any religious worshipper. He is on his own with God to come to terms with the ultimate values of life. Each Hindu is his own Socrates, Plato, St. Augustine and Bertrand Russell rolled into one!

The highest kind of education, therefore, through the Guru, is that which enables the individual to evolve himself to deeper awareness, a process of evolution from material existence to that of the spirit corresponding to the evolutionary development in biological terms, improving on the creative form of life through long aeons of experiment and survival of the best adjusted forms of that life.

Thus at the level of spirit also man slowly moves forward as he realises the need to improve to bring the atmā to the level of the Great Atmā; the level of Deity. This is his deep, just and meritful duty to achieve. To search out perfection, the realisation of the self, not the selfish self-realisation, is the objective towards which all the religions of India and their founders direct the masses. The Guru lays down the foundation on which the future construction of life depends.

Whereas Hindu thinkers lay emphasis on duties and spiritual life, they do not ignore the importance of the sentient emotional aspect of human nature. Moksha is not only the liberation of soul, but also the liberation from the functional urges which demand physical fulfilment before we move to the next station of life. Life demands strong shoulders to undertake heavy responsibilities towards our parents and grand-parents, the society and our fellow beings. The first 25 years of life are meant for education of all the essentials needed by the future. The duty of the Guru is not to impart education of the three Rs but the science of life. The student learns continence, chastity, service and devotion, and so prepares himself for the future battles of life as duty demands of him.

From 25 to 50 years of age one has to utilise all that one has learnt with the Guru. While the father retires leaving all his responsibilities to the son, the married son now fulfils the duties towards the family, the society and the rest. While Moksha is a goal of life, liberation cannot be attained, in any case, without paying off what one owes to others including parents, forefathers, one's children and the society. One owes to the ancestors and the parents because they are the originators of one's being. Man is not only the son of yesterday, he is the father of tomorrow also. He lives through the future generations and as such he continues the will of his ancestors which is his duty he can perform to the best of his mental, physical and spiritual capacity as much beautifully and dutifully as he should. Men and women, for this simple reason, are encouraged to enter married life. Monastic tendencies, characteristic of early Christians and Buddhists, have been discouraged until one has expressed the normal impulses which bring about disastrous effects if kept unhumanly supported.

Marriage

Marriage is regarded as sacred. There is nothing unholy about sex life nor is there anything guilty. Marriage is a means to the growth of spiritual life. Even the gods of the Hindus are married, and they are accompanied by their consorts. It is in marital relationship that one learns to be a slave to a common ideal when sensual urges are transformed into devotion.

The ideal of marriage has been sanctified to the extent that 'the gates of holy heaven are shut for him who dies unmarried'. It is for this reason that the law-giver allows various kinds of marriages. The Rāmāyana and the Mahābhāratā so frequently illustrate the 'Svayamvra', the marriage by one's own choice in which men of their own status were invited and the girl would choose her life partner. Or she would lay down conditions to be fulfilled intellectually or physically by the would be life-partner through performing a certain act of bravery or skill in archery or swordsmanship. Although freedom of choice is there, it has been granted only to people of equal status, attributes and background.

Marriage between people or parental **sub-caste** is not permissible nor that between the sub-caste of married sister, though of the same caste as the Kshatriya, Brahmin, Vaish etc. Such marriages are considered incestuous, and the children from such marriages are labelled as out-castes or the so called untouchables who are generations old product of castigation. Attempts are, however, being made to improve the lot of untouchables. Quite a lot has been achieved in this reform movement but there is extensive work still to do. Untouchability has been out-lawed by Indian constitution but law cannot change centuries old attitudes and customs.

Through lucky intuition and observation Hindu thinkers assumed the influence of heredity and encouraged marriage among those who approximate to the type of their own type. The caste system does not encourage indiscriminate cross-breeding. Although interbreeding has been taking place, marriage within one's own caste has been considered as sound and proper. The influence of heredity has always appealed to the Hindu mind as it did to the Greeks. Plato's view of biological selection, and Aristotle's belief that 'the state should encourage the increase of superior type' are no different from the caste system of the Hindus. The science of Eugenics rests on somewhat safer grounds. Half the chromosomes in the cells of our body come from the father and the other half from the mother and it has now been well established that they sincerely transmit the qualities and the stupidities of not only the parents but those of the great-grand parents even. If parents are of about the same class, the child would be practically the equal of the parents. Blood tells. The level of social and cultural background of the would-be partners is a sound foundation of happy life here and hereafter. All the aids of environments cannot produce a genius out of inborn stupidity, and the heritage rich or poor in conduct cannot be transformed abruptly.

Monogamy has been idealised because it is in the best interest of the family although polygamy has been tolerated under exclusive circumstances. In every case whether the bond between wife and husband is monogamous or polygamous, the ideal marriage remains indissoluble. The Rāmāyana, the Mahābhārata and the Purānas repeatedly portray the catastrophic consequences entailing the polygamus enterprise. Polygamy among the Hindus is as serious a crime as in England.

Second marriage is permissible only by consent of the first wife provided the first one is incapable of bearing children. The only ground for dissolution of the marriage is adultery, and in this case the wife forfeits every claim or right to the property or fortunes of the husband. There is no such thing as maintenance under such circumstances. In the case of second marriage by consent of the first wife, the former will maintain her status the same as prior to the second marriage.

The Hindu women have never demanded equality to the status of men be it in the society or within the walls of the house. The Hindu social norm gives them natural superiority. In a way the 'Hindu social code is more complimentary to her than him'. The Hindu wife is 'ardhāngani'—a reassuring tribute which means 'the half of the body'—the better-half. She is the owner of everything that belongs to him and rightfully exercises her full authority in the household functions, ceremonies or celebrations. Practically no important function or ceremonies like marriage of the son or daughter is complete without her.

Marriage and Horoscope

The society which holds so high and idealistic view of life companionship is bound to be cautious in deciding to choose a suitable partner. The horoscope plays an effective part in such decisions. The family background has so much to contribute to establish whether or not the couple 'shall live happily ever after'. In the world of practicalities the Aryans invented the decimal system and the mathematical rule of three, the concept of zero (the 'shunya' in Sanskrit) and the value of infinity. In fact the Arabic word for numeral is 'Hindsa' meaning 'from India'. The Aryans were also the first to chart the zodiac, to consider the rotational and gravitational influence of the planets, something which has become fundamental in launching the rockets and sending the astronauts deep into space for research during this century. This led to the profound study of science of astrology which still has a strong influence within Indian society, more so on marriage among the Hindus. Elaborate horoscopes are commonly to be found in almost every home.

For times immemorial very detailed study of the effects of the planetary system upon behaviour which shapes the conduct (and therefore the course) of a human being's life, has been taken by the Hindu cosmologists with vehement ardour. Almost every Hindu even to this day is much influenced by this system of study. When a Hindu baby is born, a janampatrikā or a horoscope is made out by the family pandit who knows the history of the family generations back, and the influence of the planets on the new-born. The janampatrikā is a scroll showing the houses of the firmament, the zodiacal changes, the houses of the moon and the sun in conjunction with other planets throughout the future years. These parchments often range from one foot to forty yards in length.

In orthodox families they are consulted mostly before any major events are undertaken (such as a long journey or a business transaction). Even many highly educated ones still follow this custom which has existed for centuries, is deeply ingrained and experienced and known to be too beneficial to be cast aside lightly. Especially for marriage the horoscope of each partner is seriously studied by the family priests, and often contemplated marriages are put off if the two horoscopes do not satisfactorily match in one aspect or the other. No matter the one who prepared the scroll is a scholar or a charlatan, the actual time and the date of birth are accurate and invariable, and are a far more valid and authenticated document than a good many passports. Families can trace their ancestry back through generations in authentic details including the family origin, etc. It can be ascertained to an extent in the case of intended marriages that the would-be partners suited each other from the point of view of heredity.

Caste System

From the beginning of her history India has been peopled by various racial groups. There have been the Aryans, the Dravidians, the yellow Mongols, the Greeks, the Persians and the Scythians. No other country on earth has had so multifarious a populace from so early a period of history as India has. At the same time we can safely say that no other country has dealt with so acute a problem so efficiently as India.

Caste originally referred to colour. While each group of people has its own well-defined colour, it also has its own specific traits, tastes and traditions which quite naturally it wanted to preserve. Some of the present day castes, therefore, are the making of the people of a group however large or small. There are castes named after professions; after the name of a part of country, the province or the village of origin; the beliefs of the group, the temperament and nicknames etc. So often people have made a caste of their own which had never been heard of. The attitude of confining oneself within one's own group is an old sociological spectacle seen alike among the most refined and the most backward people. Almost every British club is open to people of one profession or other and refuses admittance to the members of other trades, profession—or unions, etc.

In order to avoid conflict between different races and groups, Hinduism adopted as it would appear, a democratic way, and allowed every group to develop the very best in it so long as it did not hinder the course of progress of others. In the late Rig Vedic hymns the four castes i.e. the Brāhmina, the Kshatriya, the Vaishya and the Shudra are said to have sprung up from the four limbs of the Creator. The Brāhmins were born from the mouth of Brahma, the Primordial Man; the Kshatriyas from his arms; the Vaishyas from his thighs and the Shudras from his feet. It was thus demonstrated that each is the part of the whole, and that they have to function in a way most appropriate to give vitality to the body polity. It was maintained that the society could not progress harmoniously without proper division of labour. It was not something very much different from Plato's classification of men and their functions in the Utopian philosophy. H. G. Wells goes a little further in dividing the society into three rather than four classes, ignoring the fourth as the one which in his view, however, was not worthy of any attention.

In the Hindu system the Brahmina was the head of the social order but he had to pay a high price for it. His function demanded a life of study, sanctity, austerity and purity. Even for his food he had to depend on the devotion of other classes. He was required to shun worldly honour as 'he would shun poison'. Whatever the role of castes, it was made clear that one who found it difficult to fit in the devised scheme of society could leave the region and settle somewhere else if one so desired. There was no bar, in practice, to the free mobility by virtue of which a number of Vaishya and Shudra families left their place of origin and settled in other parts of the country, and rose to the status of kings if and when they deserved.

At this point there were no Chandāls, the casteless caste, an unclean savage tribe which lived in the forests in the colonies outside normal social habitation. These people had been thrown out of society due to the social misdemeanour or for intolerable crime. Gradually, as it happens in every society, through the force of hard customs the free mobility in caste evaporated and the system became rigid and more rigid still. The untouchables or the so called Chandāls became a stigma on the free spirit of Hinduism. Though every attempt is being made to ameliorate the lot of the out-castes, the field still demands extensive work.

Death and Cremation
Hindus cremate the dead body (unlike Muslims who bury their dead in ancestral grounds). There is only one sect of the Yogis in Hindu society, who bury their dead in cross-legged posture seated in salt. Although there is all love, respect and affection for the deceased, the essence is gone. The spirit

which has departed from the body has to answer for the right and wrong of the life time. There is no such thing as the Day of Judgement when the bodies will rise from graves to meet the Lord. The body is just wrapped in a simple cotton shroud and cremated while a few hymns from any of the holy books are read. Cremation of children under the age of three years or in some parts of the country five years is neither dictated nor pleaded. At this age the body of the deceased child is buried. If it is an infant of a few days or weeks, the body wrapped in a piece of cloth is gently left afloat on the surface of the water of a river or sea.

Whether the body is cremated at home or abroad it is on the fourth day from the day of cremation when the remains are collected. Traditionally the remains were taken to Haridwār where the river Ganges winds its way through. Haridwār which means 'the gateway to God' is surrounded by hills, jungles and forests known for plenteous peace, quiet and beauty. From most parts of India, Hindus of almost every caste still carry the remains of the deceased there and deposit them in the waters of the river Ganges. Here people come shocked, woebegone with broken hearts, and see the common destiny of the man in flesh, and share each other's grief. The realization that this is the end which binds all of us together, alleviates the suffering, and by the time one returns home, one regains sufficient composure and tranquillity to go ahead with life in a normal way.

The traditional visits to Haridwar whether to deposit the remains of the departed one or on account of pilgrimage have another advantage. Each family has its own priest known as a Panda settled in Haridwar. The visitor would be visited by the Panda of his clan and he would take note of the purpose of one's visit and the date and he would take the details also of other persons of the same family if they are not recorded with him. Family background—sometimes up to twenty generations are recorded with the priest without any mistake. There is no holy order subjecting one to follow the traditional course, yet from the ignorant to the intellectual all are anxious to visit there.

Ahinsā—Non-violence

Preservation of all forms of life is a duty which we should discharge by means of love, sympathy and kindness. Non-violence is a prominent feature of Hindu religion and ethics. Hinduism does not believe in the use of force under all the circumstances. Heroism and politics have their own place but love and wisdom is cherished. Greater is the one who saves, than the one who kills. Hinduism considers all life as sacred and this sanctity extends to animal and plant life also. Security of all kinds of life was one of the ten dicta during the rule of King Ashoka (circa 300 BC). It is through slow evolutionary process that man has achieved the present status of his physiological, spiritual and mental superiority. Cruel killing of animals hardens human nature and the benevolent heart turns into a hard rock. Supported by man-made creeds and institutions men 'have enslaved the rest of animal creation and have treated the distant cousins in fur and feathers so badly that beyond doubt, if they were able to formulate a religion, they would depict the Devil in human form'. Murder, slaughter, intentional killing and wounding do not fit in the frame of Hindu nature and conduct.

As a rule the Hindus are vegetarian and most of them would not eat an egg, even, and this applies to the most westernised elite. It would be hard to find a Hindu eating beef. Beef eating is as obnoxious to the Hindu as pig meat to a Muslim no matter what reason they offer for this aversion.

Conclusion

Hinduism is the spiritual repository of India but its value resides in its universal fundamentals. It does not represent the spiritual experience of any one great individual but an enlightened culture which has a complex and collective manifestation like that of the starry world. Wisdom is not associated with any particular set of theological dogmas but it has the breadth of universal soil. Various creeds may find their sustenance from its wisdom but none can set any sectarian boundaries around it.

Hinduism is an art of living not a rigid form of thought. The true 'artist is the glutton of eternity'. The more he has, the more he seeks. "Truth never is, always is 'a-being'. For the Hindu the quest is ceaseless".

Deep as we dive in the Ocean of Eternal, the new depth is always open before us. Every step further is a milestone on the road to discovery, but it is not an end in itself. Most mistaken are those who claim they have reached the bottom of the ocean, and there is nothing left to be sought after. While 'God hideth Himself', the search continues with the oldest noble prayer of the *Upanishad,*

> *From the Unreal lead me to Real,*
> *From Darkness lead me to Light,*
> *From Death lead to Immortality.*

And this sums up the Hindu aspirations.

BIBLIOGRAPHY

The Hindu View of Life, Dr. Sarvapalli Radhakrishnan; Publisher: George Allen & Unwin, London.

The Brahma Sutra—Text and Explanation, translated and with an introduction by Dr. S. Radhakrishnan; Publisher George Allen & Unwin, London.

Bhagavad Gita—Sanskrit and English version, translated by Dr. S. Radhakrishnan; Publisher: George Allen & Unwin, London.

Bhagavad Gita—Sanskrit and English version, Annie Besant, G. A. Natesan, Madras.

Hinduism, The World's Oldest Faith—Professor K. M. Sen; Pelican Books, Harmondsworth, Middlesex, 1961.

Ramayana, C. Rajgopalachari; Publisher: Bhartiya Vidya Bhavan, Chaupatty, Bombay, 1957.

Mahabharata, C. Rajagopalachari; Hindustan Times, New Delhi.

The Indian Heritage—by Professor Humayun Kabir, Asia Publishing House, London, 1946.

Hindu Society at Crossroads, K. M. Panikkar; Asia Publishing House, London.

The Holi Lake of the Acts of Rama, Tulsi Das; translated by W. D. P. Hill; Oxford University Press, 1952.

Eastern Religion and Western Thought, Dr. S. Radhakrishnan; Clarendon Press, Oxford.

The World's Greatest Religions, Special Edition. Life Magazine; Collins, London and Glasgow.

Sources of Indian Tradition, 2 volumes, introduction to Oriental Civilisations, editor Wm. Theodore de Bary; Columbia University Press, New York and London.

Thinking About Hinduism, Eric J. Sharp, Lutterworth Educational, 1971.

India, The Making of World History; Macmillan Education, 1971, Vol I; India in the Ancient World, Evan Charlton.

Hinduism, John H. Hinnells and Eric J. Sharp (Editors) et al; Oriental Press Limited, 32 Ridley Place, Newcastle upon Tyne, 1970.

Hindu and Christian in Vrindaban, Klaus Klostermaier; SCM Press, 1969.

Dharam Kumar Vohra, Hinduism in Our Religions, Ed. H. Guy; Dents Publications, 1974.

ISLAM

by Muhammad Iqbal

Preamble*

There have been Muslim residents in the British Isles for at least 150 years. The numbers were, however, not very numerous until fairly recent times.

Throughout its history the British Isles has been a refuge for small numbers of European migrants. After the Second World War large numbers of East Europeans were glad to make Britain their new home. These immigrants were primarily Christians of one denomination or another. Some, however, were Jews, and a small number were Muslims. Though life was difficult at first, language being the main barrier to integration, gradually these people learned to adapt to the British way of life, though still retaining many of their own national and religious characteristics and customs. Later the flourishing post-war British industry acted as a magnet for people outside Europe—especially those in the developing and often overcrowded countries. These people came prepared to work hard to earn the money they needed so badly, not merely for personal gain, but to provide for poorer members of the extended family back in their mother country.

Britain in her turn, short of manpower, welcomed this new intake and source of labour, many of whom were willing to work abnormal hours, and any day of the week. Such unskilled and semi-skilled workers were soon joined by other Commonwealth immigrants such as students, nurses, teachers, doctors many of whom were prepared to begin life in Britain as humble labouring people working their way up to the roles and status they had previously held in their own country. This new group of migrants, many of whom had originally intended also to return home, began to settle down. They found that they needed their families round them. So their families came. The immigration level rose rapidly until in 1962 the Commonwealth Immigrants Act reduced the intake. Further control was enforced in 1965, 1968, and 1971.

What now had happened to make these people a problem for the British nation? A European immigrant turned out of his own country will obviously be regarded differently from a young healthy Commonwealth immigrant coming because he wishes to. It was natural that sooner or later the Commonwealth immigrant would wish to share his new-found home with other members of his family. Thus, in certain industrial areas of Britain large numbers of immigrants began to settle and create communities of their own, separate and unrelated to the life pattern of the indigenous population who in

*This section is based on a talk delivered by the author at the Standing Conference on Inter-Faith Dialogue in Education, Birmingham, 24th July, 1974.

their turn moved to other areas of the city or town. The two main communities evolved in this way have been West Indian, predominantly Christian and Asian, predominantly Muslim. There are, however, many Muslims from other parts—for example, Nigerians, Malaysians, Turks, and Turkish Cypriots.

Although the West Indian Christian is obviously not British, his way of dress and many social habits conform, more or less, to those of the British way of life. The Asian Muslims, however, are not only dark skinned but have customs and social habits often quite unrelated to anything the British had previously experienced in their own country. In addition to this, great numbers of them were practising a religion, the tenets of which were little understood or even misunderstood by the indigenous population. That religion was Islam—which pervades the whole of its follower's way of life.

To be a Muslim is to practise Islam, to practise is to live, work, and pray with Muslims. It was inevitable that a Muslim community should grow and expand and wherever it grew it would be apparent that this community was Muslim.

Immigration as a whole followed the pattern of husband arriving first, joined later by his wife and family. In the case of many Muslim immigrants they came alone with the ultimate intention of returning home after a few years. Many were followed by their wives only when it was enacted that children should not come without their mother in whose absence they were not properly cared for. It was in this second stage of the family's settlement that the Muslim immigrant really began to plant his feet well into the British soil. A home had to be found and furnished and few people build up a home only to pull it apart after a couple of years. Once the idea of settling as a family was established, it was not long before other members of the family wanted to settle in Britain to be near their loved ones.

Now, a man alone can often live a life completely divorced from that of the community around, but when he has dependants to look after he soon becomes aware of the English social system. Official forms and documents can be a great worry to a man of little education and knowledge of the English language. This especially affects Muslims from Asian countries. It is easy for him to make mistakes but not so easy to avoid them or to avoid trouble, if it arises out of these mistakes. The British system, itself, rigid and law-respecting, in many ways different from systems he is used to, can cause a great deal of confusion. On such occasions a man must turn to others for help, in some cases becoming dependent upon his own children. Compulsory education means that his children must learn to speak English. In this respect many Muslim mothers were cut off from the world outside the Muslim community. It was no easy task for a woman of rural background, with, perhaps, only a shaky command of her own official language, to learn a completely new one in a strange environment. It was no wonder that many tended to cling to their own community all the more, as a refuge from the unknown. The sight of busy traffic, an experience for ladies unused to Western town and city life, is almost as traumatic as the sight of women scantily dressed, a depressing enough sight to one whose religious beliefs recommend modest attire completely covering the body.

Gradually, more and more Muslim women are learning English and playing a more active role in the life of the community, often forming their own associations and committees and helping in community relations work. Those who go out to work play a part in making friendly contacts with the host community and fostering better relationships of understanding and tolerance, though they soon find it is an extremely demanding role which does not always help to keep the family together. In these cases the oldest daughter soon finds that she must share and sometimes take over completely the responsibility for housework, including the preparation of meals. Here the community provides a valuable service, for, where the community is, there the *Halal* butcher is. He can usually provide many other foods eaten in both climates. Whenever a Muslim moves out of his community environment he finds it extremely difficult to find ritually killed meat. In the Muslim household, the meal of the day is still that of his native land. In the case of the Asian Muslim, it consists of hot curry and rice or *chuppatis* accompanied by salad and water or fruit drink followed by fruit. At meal times, especially in the morning and evening, he will give thanks to *Allah the Almighty*. By this example he can guide his children on the path of Islam.

A major worry for Muslim parents is the fact that their children soon begin to adopt English standards and ideas. They start to question not only traditional customs but religious ideas which seem to be strangely alien to life in a Western materialistic society. Islam is not something which can be learnt and adhered to overnight. It must be lived, breathed and fostered until it cannot be separated from life itself. It requires constant practice, and it is this fact that creates the dilemma for a Muslim parent in Britain today. Most Muslims acknowledge that Britain is a fair place to live, and in many ways they have come to depend upon it for their livelihood, but it is hard to judge how possible it is to live as a Muslim within the society as a whole. Many are prepared to try to do so, in the belief that Islam will survive all tests. Already many old terrace houses have been converted into mosques and many devout and concerned Muslims act as *Imams* or 'religious leaders'. They lead the congregations in prayer, perform religious ceremonies at births and deaths, teach *Arabic* texts and ideas of Islam to young Muslims. Other educated Muslims help them in this task which increasingly requires people well-versed in the English language. Many parents do not insist upon traditional Muslim dress, but most Muslims wish their children to wear trousers of some kind to cover the legs. For girls attending mixed schools it is especially important that they are clothed properly, and though they may have to conform to colour and cloth of school uniforms, they have usually been successful in maintaining the trousers as part of their way of life.

The mixing of the sexes in and out of school at the *adolescent stage* is not a matter easy to be categorical about, but this kind of social contact is contrary to the *ethos* of Islamic teaching. And a thorough appreciation of the Islamic principles involved is, therefore, needed, especially during the adolescent years leading to marriage. It should be appreciated that in spite of any tendency for the young to accept new and alien social customs, the final influence still lies in the hands of the Muslim family.

These family influences are still quite strong. In this respect the families still adhere to the set Islamic ceremonies. Marriages are arranged between Muslims. New born babies hear the call to the prayers and the boys are circumcised. Funerals are simple and carried out in accordance with the *Sunnah* of the Prophet Muhammad. The togetherness of the true spirit of brotherhood in Islam and the closeness of family relationship are still very strong. How long the family will remain at the centre of young people's lives will depend entirely upon the extent to which adult Muslims wish to see their *Faith* revitalised in a non-Muslim environment. For, in a world where a man is encouraged to be the individual and get whatever he can, it takes a firm religious *Faith* to follow the commands of one's *Maker* rather than the dictates of *self*. In short, the flourishing existence of the Muslim Community in Britain depends entirely upon every Muslim in Britain today. He is not only to believe in Islam but to practise those beliefs, as it is enjoined by his *Faith,* thus setting an example for all to see and acknowledge.

> *"And unto thee have We revealed the Scripture with the truth confirming whatever Scripture was before it and a watcher over it. So judge between them by that which Allah hath revealed, and follow not their desires away from the Truth which hath come unto thee.*
>
> *"For each We have appointed a divine Law and traced out-way. Had Allah willed, He could have made you one community. But that He may try you by that which he has given you (He hath made you as ye are). So, vie one another in good works. Unto Allah ye will all return, and He will then inform you of that wherein ye differ."*
>
> *—(Al-Qur'ān 5:48)*

And what are the Muslim's Scripture and practices, we will examine them in detail in the ensuing pages.

The Belief

لَا اِلٰهَ اِلَّا اللّٰهُ مُحَمَّدٌ رَّسُوْلُ اللّٰهِ

'There is no deity but Allah...and Muhammad is his Messenger.'

Of all the world's universal religions Islam is the last in historical development, coming into existence in the 7th Century after Christ's birth. For those who profess to be Muslim it is the most clearly defined. It is at the same time the most clearcut religion to follow—hence its widespread appeal to people of all nations. The Arabic word ISLAM[1] literally means 'Submission to the Will of God', and MUSLIM[2] means 'one who submits'. Mr Barkat Ali, Chief Editor, *Dar-ul-Ehsan,* has enlarged upon this, pointing out that it is not only submission. Islam actually means a system which 'enables a Muslim to get into a state of peace and the state free from vice and defect; also it enables him to cause all kinds of peace to others. The message of Islam reminds men of endless possibilities and his boundless capabilities, and places in front of him some fundamental truths of science in order to open up a way for his progress and understanding. For instance it tells him that he can go to other planets[3] and there are atmospheres and gases on other planets[4] that the planets float in their orbits.'[5]

Islam bows down in worship to a single all-powerful God,[6] Allah, Who manifested Himself through the Archangel Gabriel to the last and seal of the prophets, Muhammad (may Allah bless and preserve him) who was, according to tradition, born in Mecca in AD 570. This revelation which was miraculously sustained over a period of years, was taken down by Muhammad's followers on 'scraps of parchment and leather, camels, shoulder-blades and ribs, pieces of board and the hearts of men,' and collected into 114 chapters called *suras,* which have been compiled into the Muslim *Holy Book.*

This outpouring of divine inspiration through the medium of the great Prophet is called the *Qurān* (meaning a reading). It is the repository of all the truth about life, all that a Muslim must do as a human being in this world, how he must order his family life, his finances and what he passes on as inheritance, his eating habits, his moral codes. These are very strictly defined and the *Qurān* is accepted as the last and final[7] revelation of Allah on the ordering of human life. This intensity, and the concentrated worship it has inspired, has created a self-contained culture and a self-sustaining civilisation stronger than in any other faith—its goal is human success in this life as well as in the next.

Although there is a common ancestry to both Christianity and Islam, there are fundamental differences in the concept of Godhead—to a Muslim Allah is indivisible and there is no sense of the Trinity of the Christian God. There are, however, many meeting points between Islam and Christianity. The *Qurān* is the actual Word of the indivisible God in much the same way as those words of

Christ spoken directly to his disciples in the New Testament. The difference lies in the fact that the former is the final and unchanged Word, whereas the Bible has undergone change and critical analysis. The *Qurān* is the collection of revelations made to Muhammad through the Archangel Gabriel. In this sense Muhammad can be said to be the interpreter of Allah's message. Direct confrontation with God came in later Muslim development in the magnificent singing poetry of the Sufi mystics.

In Persia in the 9th Century ascetics known as *Sufis* (wool wearers—*Suf* means wool) retired from the world into monasteries or wandered the roads creating a new tradition of mystic poetry, which sang with intense out-pouring and joyousness of mystical union with God. This ecstatic state of religious faith came into existence when Muslim culture responded to the Greco-Roman Byzantine and Persian heritage and the influence of other world religions.

The ascetics of those days and the present time are, however, all required to abide by and practise the teachings of the *Qurān* and Muhammad's sayings if they claim to be Muslims. There are only a small number of ultra-spiritualists among the followers of Islam. To lead a successful life requires striking a balance[8] between extremities. Perhaps it will not be out of place to mention here the novel behaviour of the ascetics. An act done by a Muslim mystic might appear to be wrong according to the dictates of the holy *Qurān* and *Hadith* but in fact may be in conformity with it in the mystic codes.[9]

One instance is the case of Al-Hallaj who rose to such a stage of Sufism that he broke the traditional barriers and declared himself God, which the Islamic jurists of that day challenged there and then. For this breach he was persecuted and finally executed in Baghdad in AD 922.

Islam has in fact *never* encouraged its followers to resign the worldly life in order to engage in such exclusively individual meditative pursuits. Such mystical union with the Creator is regarded as coming *last of all* in a man's religious development which begins essentially with orthodox traditional practice of the basic tenets of Islam.

Muhammad's ascension[10] into Heaven through piety and love of mankind has, of course, been the virtuous inspiration for Sufi belief. But this is only one of many aspects of his life. A Muslim who follows Muhammad in all the many facets of his life can surely aspire to be distinguished amongst mankind and near to the Creator.

The following Chapter[11] of Sincerity, *a Sura* (Chapter) from the *Qurān,* is what the average Muslim should keep most in mind, and exemplifies the essential truth of the Muslim view of the definition of the Creator.

> *'In the name of Allah, the Beneficent, the Merciful!*
> *Say: He is Allah, the One!*
> *Allah, the eternally Besought of all!*

He begetteth not, nor was begotten.
And there is none comparable unto Him.'

—(112th Chapter of Sincerity from the Qurān
—Picthall Translation)

The Historical Background

Much of the teaching of the Old Testament and the general understanding of the creation of mankind from Adam and Eve has been handed down to the followers of Islam. A Muslim firmly believes that these are the outcome of religious revelations and injunctions communicated to the Prophets from time to time.[12] The Holy Sermons of Muhammad clearly accept the *Scrolls* of Moses, the *Psalms* of David and the *Gospel* of Jesus as books sent by God to the prophets in a set chronological order. One great festival[13] of the Islamic year, *Eid-ul-Adha,* sometimes spelled *Zuha* in English, in fact is done in remembrance of Abraham's near sacrifice of Ishmael (Christians believe it was Isaac), his son. Revealed books or prophets, other than those specifically mentioned in the *Qurān,* are not recognised.

From the Muslim point of view the founders of Hinduism and Buddhism and the authors of the Hindu *Vedas* and the Buddhist *Canon* can neither be accepted nor rejected categorically as Prophets in the sense that Christ is accepted along with Moses, Elija and Abraham as Prophet of the One Indivisible God.

Moreover, the authenticity of the Divine *Books* of the *Old Testament* referred to in the *Qurān* constituted the beginnings[14] of Islam. These books, other than the *Qurān,* have undergone many changes, having been handed down under the prevailing circumstances of oral traditions during long historical times, and they are far from their original forms. But the striking resemblance of certain narrations in these books, however, are strong enough points to prove their divine source.

The story of Abraham's sacrifice, for instance, in both the *Old Testament* and the *Qurān* prove its authenticity and trustworthiness. Some of the four-thousand-year-old beliefs, teachings and practices of Judaism are again akin to those of Muslims and hence the authenticity of their basis. Circumcision and ritual slaughter of animals for human consumption are common to both Jew and Muslim.

The *Qurān* is complete to a Muslim as the revelation of God,[15] and one who knows the general methods of its compilation and the presentation of its teachings will begin to understand that there are no deletions or additions. The *Qurān,* which was revealed in Arabic[16] (the subtlety of which can never be given proper justice by the more concise English translations) is complete in all respects and provides systematic guidelines of a fundamental nature to all kinds of people,[17] no matter what their nationality, at all times in history.

The Spread of Islam

Like Christianity, Islam is a proselytising[18] Faith. So great was the revelation in meaning to Muhammad the Prophet that he undertook the ordinance to spread its word and the teachings of Allah's inspiration to the pagan tribes of Saudi Arabia where he was born.

Alongside the *Qurān,* there grew up a collection of Muhammad's sayings (explanations of the revelations of Allah, and temporal matters—about 10,000 reports altogether) which have supplemented the *Qurān* to a great degree.

These are known as the *Hadith* (pronounced *Hadees).* In any problematical situation or personal moral crisis reference can be made not only to the *Qurān* but to this whole tradition of juridical interpretation.

These have been the basis for the strong impetus to take the message of Allah all over the globe. In the initial stages Islam was preached among (a) heathens, (b) Jews and (c) Christians. The pagan tribes in Mecca, Saudi Arabia, were idol worshippers and polytheists. They accepted in multitudes the message of the Great Prophet in bettering the order of society which prevailed at the time. One has to remember the context in which Islam emerged amid the feuding tribes of Arabia, in a backward uneducated desert society where there was much ignorance and apathy towards any spiritual life.

'Virility', which helped each Arab to inculcate in himself the qualities to defend himself and his tribe, was prevalent all over the society of old Arabia. Justice was indeed rough justice, hardly tempered with mercy, a case of 'an eye for an eye, a tooth for a tooth.'[19]

The *Qurān* arrived with the impact of a thunderbolt, giving the Arabs a code to 'do good and forbid evil.'[20] For the first time forgiveness or pardoning is recommended as a counter-balance for their harsh code of summary justice. Muhammad taught that man is created in the image of God who has various and manifold images. This is where the uniqueness of human character both in shape and mind is apparent, and the quality of the relationship of each human individual with God is manifested. This has influenced the attitude of Muslims towards the government and the role of the State.

The Building-up of an Islamic Society

The head of an Islamic State, it is ordained according to the ideal, must be the humblest and the most knowledgeable of all the subjects and is regarded as the servant of the people, enjoying the same equal rights as they do—but no more according to positions of status. Islam rejects the age-old conception of special privileges for the Head of State. As a matter of fact the early *Khalifahs* (the Caliphs) of Muhammad—The Apostle of God—who ruled the vast lands consisting of existing Saudi Arabia and areas from the countries around her left historic and practicable traditions for the Muslim Kings devout to the cause of Islam in times to come.

Abu-Bakr, the first Caliph, was known as the man of two pins, because he always wore a single garment which he used to pin together. Umar-b-Alkhitab, the second Caliph, who ruled the world in its entirety had the treasures of Chosroes and Caesar at his disposal but lived on bread and olive oil and wore clothes with innumerable patches. Uthman, the third Caliph, used to carry faggots of firewood on his shoulders and once, when he was asked the reason he did so, simply said, 'I wanted to know if my soul would refuse.'

When Ali succeeded, he maintained the ascetic tradition of his predecessors and is said to have bought a shirt for five Dirhams (coinage system) and finding the sleeves too long caught hold of a cobbler's knife and cut off the sleeves level with the tips of his fingers. This served to set an example of discipline and self-abnegation for those in positions of authority, especially in the beginnings of Muslim society when so much that had existed before Muhammad was based on total privilege.

The Idea of Equality
A remarkable feature of Islamic ideology is the principle of 'balance'. Islam has laid down the general rule of adopting the middle path in man's outlook as well as in his actions. To a Muslim, other religions seem to appear one-sided—sacrificing either this world or the next. Islam tries to strike a happy balance between the demands of this world and the requirements of the next. Fundamentally Islam is concerned with a spiritual democracy, so much so that there has never been a priestly hierarchy or a dynasty of religious leaders who might act as intermediaries between man and God. The *Imam,* or prayer leader, is not the equivalent of the Christian priest. In each mosque he is responsible only to himself and not to a bishop, or to a body of the Church. Even in Islamic society, the ideal is a classless social order in which the only criterion for preference and superiority is that of character.[21] The *Holy Qurān* says:

> *"O mankind! We created you from a single (pair) of a male and a female and made you into nations and tribes that ye may know each other (not that ye may despise each other). . . . . ."*
>
> —*(Al-Qurān 49:13)*

Besides grouping into nations and tribes, Nature herself has also exercised a kind of discrimination in mental, physical and hence social inequality of human beings. Consequently, the varying degrees of intelligence, strength and

40

wealth resulted in the one being superior to the other. The science of ethnology developed in the 19th Century when also the political growth of colonisation through science and technology was soaring high, supported this view and established the superiority of the white race. The major exponent was *Julian Huxley,* whose first man is half-man and half-ape, contrary to the Muslim belief that the first man the Prophet Adam, himself, was a complete man physically furnished with psychic powers. In present times, however, the famous anthropologist, *Hector,* maintains that varying shades of skin colour have assigned no superior or peculiar characteristics to one person or another.

Division into races as mentioned in the *Holy Qurān* (49:13) has been for no other reason than to reveal the diversified nature of God's creatures and make us see that despite all differences, in the eyes of God we are equal. Only in goodness, piety and generosity may we rise in supremacy. Islam offers equal opportunity to acquire all these character traits without any regard for colour, race, sex or inheritance. On the day of the conquest of Mecca, the Prophet Muhammad declared:

> *"O Quraish! God has delivered you from pre-Islamic haughtiness and boasting about your forefathers. All people are descendants of Adam and Adam was created from dust".*

The Prophet Muhammad's famous *Farewell Pilgrimage Address* is still preserved as the best fourteen-centuries-old human rights code for the modern man. This proclaimed the rights of women over men and vice versa. Islam has lived up to the *Qurānic* dictates right up to the present day. European women were given the right to property only fifty years ago. Muslim women have enjoyed this right ever since the birth of Islam. Economic opportunities for women are immense and social protections are numerous (see section on the *System of Morality—Muslim Women).*

The Prophet Muhammad offered the world the elixir against the racial strifes and national rivalries in the brotherhood of mankind. His universally humanist sayings are but the balm for the nations suffering from the malignant and cancerous ailment of apartheid. The Prophet said:

> *"All creatures of God form the family of God and he is the best loved of God who loveth best His creatures."*
> *"O Lord! Lord of my life and of everything in the Universe! I affirm that all human beings are brothers unto one another."*
> *"Respect the ways of God and be affectionate to the family of God."*

In the *Farewell Pilgrimage Address* it was mentioned that no Arab was superior to a non-Arab except on the grounds of piety. Thus obliterating the distinction of the basis of race.

The way to this *Address* was paved during his life time, beginning from the early days when the *Quraishites,* the haughty tribesmen refused to attend the prayer assemblies with *Bilal,* the negro; *Salman,* the Persian; *Shoail,* the Roman and *Amar,* all of whom were slaves. Later *Bilal* was appointed the ruler of Medina to look after the affairs of the City. The Prophet often requested *Bilal* to sweeten the Prophet's heart by singing the *Call to Prayers. Bilal* had previously been a negro slave. He had accepted Islam, was bought by *Abu Bakr,* the first Caliph of Islam, and set free. He was very near and dear to the Prophet. It is perhaps interesting to note that not many people know the reason why the Prophet asked *Bilal* to sing the *Call to Prayers.* He had not the sweetest of voices, also he was a stammerer. But he had the greatest devotion to Islam, so much so that the Prophet was tuned to his recitation alone. Once, the Prophet was late for the congregational prayers in the mosque. The people asked him if he had not heard the call. The Prophet answered: "No, but *Bilal* did not make it." When the Prophet died *Bilal* moved away from the City, so great was his grief.

Al-Bukhari, the famous traditionalist, reports of *Gaber Ibn Abdullah,* saying, "The Prophet stood up and so did we when a funeral procession passed by. We said to the Prophet, 'O Messenger of Allah! It is the funeral of a Jew.' The Prophet replied, 'Is it not also a soul? If you see a funeral you must stand up.' " The same man also quotes *Abu Zar Al-Ghaffari,* an economic friend of the Prophet, arguing with a slave in the Prophet's presence. *Abu Zar* got irate at one stage and called him the 'son of a black woman'. As soon as he uttered these words, the Prophet looked at him and said: "This is too much, the son of a white woman is not superior to that of a black woman except in good deeds." Hearing this, *Abu Zar* laid his head on the ground and told the negro to tread upon his cheek.

Racial inequality seems to have been annihilated gradually but perseveringly throughout Muslim history. An Arab Bedouin who had trodden upon the cloak of the *Prince of Ghassan, Jabir Ibn Al-Ayhaun,* during the rites of pilgrimage, was slapped by the Prince. He complained to *Umar,* the Second Caliph of Islam, for ill-treatment at the hands of the Prince who consequently had to submit to the Caliph's order which was such that the victim was given the chance to slap the Prince in the same way as he had been slapped. The Caliph remarked to the Prince: "Islam made you one with him: and you can have no superiority over him except in piety and good works." *Umar* cautioned him further: "Since when have you enslaved people who were born free according to Islam!"

Ali, the Fourth Caliph of Islam, is reported to have said: "I am ashamed to enslave a person who says, 'Allah is my God' ". Once *Ali* sent a young servant to bring two pieces of cloth for himself and the youth. When he returned with the cloth he gave it to *Ali* who gave the better quality material to the servant and kept the other cheaper piece for himself saying: "You are a young man who may fancy to appear well-dressed, but I am old".

According to the Prophet Muhammad: "There are no genealogies in Islam." After him, the first four Caliphs, *Abu Bakr, Umar, Uthman* and *Ali,* discriminated one group of people from another purely on the basis of religious devotion. This is the reason why the off-spring of the Prophet came to be respected because, genealogically, they belonged to the fountainhead of Islam and were therefore considered to be more pious than the others. In latter days, in order to command worldly respect and recount their worth to others, people claimed to be descendants of famous Arab tribes and invented such names as *Ansari, Hashmi, Quraishi, Siddiqui, Uthmani* and *Alvi. Umar bin Abdul Aziz* (717-720 C.E.), the *Umayyid* Caliph, put an end to such ill practices by appointing the talented non-Arabs to the highest paid offices of *Qadhi* (the Judge).

Muslim political democracy has been defined as 'the Government of God for the people by the people.' The ruler is required to carry out the commands of the *Holy Qurān* and *Hadith,* and the ability to do so is the only reason for placing the ruler above others. When Islam emphasises the sovereignty of God it means that no human being has the right to rule over other human beings.

Through Muhammad, pagan society was therefore totally transformed. Morality and piety were merged into each other, and the later influence of Sufism refined and selectively added to its credit by taking on itself the intense personal mystic love of God as the basic vehicle of all actions done for God's sake.

The moral degeneration and corruption in all aspects of life among the Arab pagans in the 6th-7th centuries AD required a mentor and a prophet of excellent example and of a resolute character.[22] The dire situation, morally and materially, demanded the exemplary behaviour of converts at the beginning and force was of course used when the first followers of Muhammad were attacked by the outraged merchants, who thrived on the pilgrim trade to Mecca where pagan believers worshipped at the shrine of the *Kaaba* (a cube shaped construction). This rectangular structure contained certain idols and a black meteorite which had fallen there from the heavens.

Persecution of the newly formed Muslim groups in Mecca, in fact caused them to flee to Medina. Upon this pagan base, Muhammad the Prophet under the inspiration of Allah, achieved something only short of the miraculous in creating a framework within which a whole people turned from polytheism and idolatry to the inner spiritual devotion directed towards one indivisible God—an all-Ruling, all-Directing Allah, at the same time very real to the worshipper. It is now to a transformed *Kaaba,* that Muslims from all over the world make their annual pilgrimage to Mecca.

'*Fight in the way of Allah, against those who fight against you, but do not begin hostilities. Allah loveth not aggressors',* says the *Qurān*[23]. This may have become the basis for *Jehad,* Holy War, which many Muslims feel is misinterpreted in Western history books, for the spread of Islam has taken place peaceably during recent centuries.

Islam now has a gigantic number of followers. Between one quarter and one fifth of the world's population is Muslim—ie, more than 950,000,000 people. They are spread over China, Indonesia, Africa and even America and the Caribbean. It is estimated that there are about 1.5 million Muslims in Britain. Incidentally, the great strength of the Muslim Faith is its very sincere and staunch belief in the brotherhood of man without any sense of colour or race. For this reason the highest rate of conversions is amongst Negro populations, both in Africa and the USA. Islam in fact embraces different sociological, climatic, cultural and political conditions. Muslims sometimes retain these strong influences even if of insignificant importance.

For instance, although disapproved, many superstitions still exist at rural level, which do not, in fact, have any sanction in Islamic tenets of Faith. Setting out on a journey towards the North on a Tuesday or Wednesday is still considered to be attendant with misfortune and bad luck. The same is thought to be so if a black cat walks across the road at the start of a journey. These are superstitions acquired from a common culture at the village level during the long years of Muslim and Hindu living together in one society, and have become diffused throughout Muslim society, which had its ancestry in the India/Pakistan sub-Continent. Similar phenomena can be observed in Christianity.

It was not until the 10th and 11th Centuries AD when regular missionaries were sent out and the Arab traders and travelling Muslims in other countries came into contact with non-Muslims, that a great majority of non-Muslims accepted Islam. The Prophet Muhammad died in the year AD 632 and the spread of Islam after him took place under the rule of political empires, ie, the Caliphates of *Rashidins, Umayyids, Abbasids* and *Ottomans.* Muslim rule became established in major areas of the world, such as undivided India, Spain, East and South East Asia, and Africa. All over the Muslim world, except for the knowledge of at least the bare essential amount of Arabic used in prayers, the teaching of Islam is carried out in the native vernaculars and abundant literature is available in the major languages of the world.

Muhammad—The Prophet of Islam
Muhammad (peace be upon him) was born in August, AD 570 at Mecca, Saudi Arabia. As descendants of Abraham, through Ishmael, the Arabs of those

days had but a vague idea of a Supreme God. The *Kaaba,* the House of God, was full of idols. The promotion of artistic and scientific knowledge was at a standstill and the people were under the grip of vices such as gambling, drinking of intoxicants, female infanticide, slavery, illegitimate relationships, cheating and intertribal strife. The Arabic language was, however, rich in both prose and poetry, and Arab hospitality was exceptionally good.

Muhammad's father, Abdullah had died even before his birth and his grandfather undertook his upbringing. Muhammad lost his mother at the age of six, his grandfather at the age of eight and was eventually left under the care of an uncle. He was a sensitive young man who was given to wandering off into the desert to fast and meditate. It was under such conditions in fact, that the Archangel Gabriel appeared to him and said, 'Recite'.[22]

Thus the *Qurān* came into being. He grew to be a pious man and was recognised as *'El-Ameen'*—the Trusty and the Faithful.

Besides the household jobs he used to do for his uncle he was employed as a trade agent by Khadeejah, a wealthy Meccan widow. She received favourable reports of his behaviour and professional knowledge and skill and sent him her offer of marriage. At the age of 25 he married Khadeejah, who was then forty. The marriage was a happy one and she bore him four daughters—Fatima being one of them. At the age of forty Muhammad had a Divine Call to the prophethood. The first few who accepted Islam were his wife, *Ali, Zaid* and *Abu-Bakr.*

The Prophet migrated to Yathrib, now known as Medina, in the year AD 622 because of opposition in his home town, but a great deal of goodwill was present amongst the inhabitants who had accepted Islam during the pilgrimage to the *Kaaba.* The Meccans tried to harass them even there and a number of battles of great historical significance was fought.

Hijrat—The Beginning of the Muslim Calendar

The flight to Yathrib was known as the *Hijrat* (flight) and it is from this date, AD 622, that all Muslim calendars are dated. Yathrib was later named *Madinat-an-Nabi* (City of the Prophet) now known as Medina. *Hijrat* (the migration of the Prophet from Mecca to Medina) is interpreted as an ever-living reminder to the Muslims that mere geographical ties meant nothing to him.

Muhammad died in the year AD 632 at the age of sixty-three and, though he had married several times, he left no male issue. Whoever claims to be his descendant claims through Fatima and her two sons Hassan and Hussain.

The collection and compilation of the Divine revelations received during 23 years in the form of the *Holy Qurān* was done by Uthman the third Caliph. Muhammad himself had left the outlines for his followers to edit afterwards.

Muhammad was the most excellent example of the embodiment of human and angelic characteristics.[23] The detailed study of his life history establishes this without a doubt. (It is interesting to note that Christ was born of brown complexion whereas the descriptions given of Muhammad mention a red and white complexion, with long arched eyebrows divided by a vein which throbbed visibly in moments of passion). In the words of the well-known historian, Lane-Poole:

> *'He was of the middle height, rather thin, but broad of shoulders, wide of chest, strong of bone and muscle. His head was massive, strongly developed. Dark hair, slightly curled, flowed in a dense mass down almost to his shoulders. Even in advanced age it was sprinkled by only about twenty grey hairs. . . His face was oval-shaped. . . Great black restless eyes shone out from under long, heavy eyelashes. His nose was large, slightly aquiline—His teeth upon which he bestowed great care, were well set, dazzling white. . . A full beard framed his manly face. His skin was clear and soft, his complexion red and white, his hands were as silk and satin. . . His step was quick and elastic; yet firm and as that of one who steps from a high to a low place. In turning his face he would also turn his full body. His whole gait and presence were dignified and imposing. His countenance was mild and pensive. His laugh was rarely more than a smile.'*

At the time of his death a considerable number of non-Muslims had accepted Islam. These followers like to be called Muslims rather than Muhammadans, because Muhammad at all times wished to make it clear that he was a God-sent Prophet, a human being[24] interpreting the Divine Allah, the Beneficent, the Merciful; therefore the religion should not be named after him. Muslims never refer to the name 'Muhammad' alone, but always add 'Peace be on him'.

Observance of Islam—Daily Life

A Muslim has a set of systematic rules to order his life. These are known as the Five Pillars of Islam and are described later. This might give rise to the thought that life is governed by rigid laws with ensuing difficulties as Muslims are transferred into alien societies concerned with worldly progress, and the necessary adjustments to industrial and technological demands. But the case is otherwise. A high degree of flexibility exists and so long as the end is based on goodwill the means are quite often immaterial. For example, allowance is made for saying the prayers in the home, or in the open air under certain circumstances, although the Prophet always insisted on saying prayers in the mosque in order to bring to everyone's notice the sense of equality, unity and brotherhood among Muslims.

a. Interpretation of Religious Injunctions

Within Islam there is little chance, either at the one extreme, of political materialism taking hold in society or, at the other end, of an other-worldly mystical philosophy becoming part of the individual approach to God.

There are many specific injunctions to what a Muslim must follow in his earthly and daily life and the remarkable thing is that on the whole, no matter where a Muslim finds himself, he will try to ensure that they are carried out in his actual living.

Islam is very definitely opposed to any political 'isms' which are in conflict with the concept of *Tauheed* (unification of God) and *Tawakkal* (Trust in God). The concept of *Tauheed,* the principle of Unity, has had a profound effect upon Muslim thought and social ethics. The philosophy which lies behind it is that unity manifests itself in the realm of the natural world.[25] Islam regards the entire cosmos as a unity; it has been created by one God and all its different components are inter-related and they function for the achievement of one purpose—that is to praise the grandeur[26] of God. This singleness of purpose makes the world a moral order.

At the level of society this principle of unity has influenced Muslim thinking more dramatically on the concept of the brotherhood of man. This is no idle term. According to Islam, all human beings form one family. Islam thus refutes the idea of racial superiority, and it is to the eternal credit of Islam that it has quite genuinely and freely lived up to this ideal. Race and colour are of no concern to a Muslim. From the other-worldly point of view the Sufi tradition, although it has had a profound effect on deeply religious Muslims, is not in the majority and is not acceptable to some Muslims. However, among these particular followers of Islam, many men of perfect and absolute authority over religious doctrines have left a lasting influence upon the Arts and Sciences, a dividend of modern thinking in Islamic development.

Saiyedena Hazrat Ghuas-ul-Azam Abu-Muhammad Abdul Qadir (470-561 AH, after the Hijra in AD 622) was a great preacher and exponent of Islamic doctrines as well as being a Sufi mystic. He occupies a unique position among Muslim jurists. He was called, for short, *Mohiyyuddin,* that is Reviver of Religion. He delivered his sermons from a monastery in Baghdad and his principal disciples always heard him from a considerable distance in the outskirts of the city. Once a clergyman, it is said, directed in a dream by Christ to go from Yemen to meet the *Hazrat* in Baghdad and there accept Islam from his teachings, declared his dream at one of the assemblies in that city to prove the *Hazrat's* high rank among mystics.

Whether a layman would understand this cannot be vouched but the spiritualistic side of the Muslim Faith is for those who have the calling and the sensitivity for it, just as in any other faith. Sir Oliver Lodge writes in his book *The Reality of a Spiritual World* (page 12): 'The basic conclusion to which I have been led, is that a spiritual world is a reality, that there are many orders and grades of being, that the human spirit continues, that there is no inseparable barrier between different orders of existence and that under certain conditions intercommunion is possible'. These words acknowledge what most mystics feel, a unity of faith in God, the One. This is universally acknowledged as true. But for life in the ordinary day to day affairs, and for the practical purposes of the laymen, the interpretation of the *Qurān* and *Hadith* are grouped into the following grades:

1. Obligatory; such as the Five Pillars of Islam.
2. Recommended but not obligatory; such as hospitality to strangers and kindness to neighbours.
3. Indifferent; such as the looking after family pets such as cats.
4. Disapproved but not forbidden; divorce.
5. Prohibited; drinking of alcohol and eating pork meat.

b. Fundamentals of Islam

Different schools of *Fiqh* (Islamic jurisprudence) have developed because of differing interpretations and explanations of the *Qurān* and the *Hadith*. The categorising and grouping of these ordinances has brought about a major division into two sects in Islam, the *Shias* and the *Sunnis*. This is much the same as has happened in other religions which are equally rich in doctrinal and theological principles.

The *Qurān* is not a work of voluminous size, but it definitely describes in more detail than any other religious Holy Book the essential points and details of life that have to be maintained and honoured. Those matters which have been omitted and which could not have been included due to the changing circumstances of life which arise from scientific and technological development (birth control, for instance), are dealt with after agreed mutual consultations based upon equitable and non-controversial judgments, and within the framework of the *Qurān* and *Hadith*.

There is the exemplary story, for instance, of Muāz. Muhammad appointed him *Qazi* (Judge) of the Yemen and asked him about his criteria for giving judgments. Muāz said that he would look in to the *Qurān* first and if he failed to find a precedent there, he would look in the *Hadith*. If he failed even there he would then exercise his own judgment. Muhammad approved of this.

All new problems have been tackled upon such lines. During the passage of historical time different schools of jurisprudence developed— *Hanafi, Maliki, Shafei* and *Hanbali* (all four follow the *Sunni* persuasion).

The great *Imams* (religious leaders) of *Sunni, Shia* and other sects are equally revered and their interpretations of the *Qurān* and the *Hadith* remain fundamentally the same, only differing at certain points in matters of degree or detail.

Muslims from Islamic states who have been transplanted into Christian surroundings will naturally stick fervently to their own religious persuasion but at the same time will be inclined to hammer out some of the cultural disparities subject of course to the proper safeguard of their ethical codes.

Local Authority Departments and even private individuals in places where overseas populations concentrate and where multiple religious denominations now exist, have an uphill task in understanding the opposing views sometimes put forward to the same problem, and in finding a satisfactory solution without offending any one section of these communities, as well as the host community.

It is difficult for the British to comprehend the subtleties of differences *within* the Asian or West Indian communities—but they are there as they are even in the most homogeneous society. It is very easy to put all Pakistanis, all Indians in a category and to label them as one, but there are differences of opinion even among themselves. The best thing in the circumstances is to elicit the views of a cross-section of the orthodox members of the immigrant community because these are the people who can explain the pattern of living as experienced in the country of origin, and the problems of adjustment that arise under new conditions. They can act as a channel of communication between the host and Muslim community, because they know the relationship of Islamic law to everyday life even in this country. Not all official interpreters used by local authorities and police are necessarily competent. They may be more attuned to the British way of life than their own, and fail to relate the problems and pressures of the incoming village communities whose religious requirements demand a more orthodox outlook, which they themselves have relinquished long ago.

Muslim immigrants (practising or non-practising) all have at least to believe in a number of fundamental principles of Islam which are the hallmark of the Muslim. These are known as the Five Pillars of FAITH. The answer to such questions as how many of them practise them, or how far do they practise them is subject to many factors. The strange environment and the struggle to fit into it, or even to surpass the others in a changing mode of life naturally disorientate some members. Many of the men are alone and far away from their families. But such factors are only marginal and do not influence a devout Muslim who would practise the following in his own humble way.

THE FIVE PILLARS OF FAITH

1. Faith in Allah

Whoever proclaims with real reverence: *'La ilaha illallah Muhammad-ur-Rasool-lullah'*—There is no deity but Allah; Muhammad is His Messenger!—that person is a Muslim. . . This Arabic formula is termed as

Kalimah and is oft repeatēd irrespective of time and place. It is a common and repeated utterance from a Muslim of any understanding of his Faith.

In addition to the essential belief in the one God[27] and in Muhammad, His Prophet, the Muslim also believes in God's Prophets,[28]His Books,[29]Angels and Destiny (that God ordains events) and resurrection after death.

Kalimah

The world of Islam today consists of individuals, families, tribes, races, nations and states. Every nation is possessed with the idea of nationalism and one nation has been a threat to the peace of another. It has been impossible to maintain unity or brotherhood. Moreover no one nation has ever enjoyed territorial or linguistic homogeneity and 'peace has, therefore, been a short interlude between wars in the history of mankind'. So rightly commented Sir Winston Churchill. The proclamation of *Kalimah* insists on one God and one Prophet and the nationalism is defined in the Qurānic verse as 'Humanity has made one single nation.'[30]This idealistic universal brotherhood is realised through the common ideology—*The Holy Qurān.*

The *Kalimah* rejects political sovereignty of man and instead confirms God's superiority. In recent years dishonest ruling hands have made it a fast-fading reality. Under the inspiration of *Kalimah* the human mind endeavours to coincide the law[31] with morality[32] and to approach in material terms the highest office in the state (which used to be called Caliphate—the Vice-regency of God on Earth). One of these Caliphates came into the possession of Caliph Umar who obeyed the commands of the *Qurān* to the full and flogged to death his son who had committed adultery.[33] According to the *Quran*[34] 'each party to the fornication must be flogged with hundred stripes'.

The *Kalimah* divests a man of the idea of ownership and inculcates in him the habit of sharing his extra wealth with others. Thus the idea of almsgiving, *Khairat,* and *Zakāt* came into existence. It discourages hatred and prejudice.

In the heyday of Islam, *Kalimah* created a culture based on simple living, equal participation of effort, and a general reaping of benefits for the whole of society. The cultures of imperial Arabs of Damascus and Cordova, the Turkish Emperors, the Great Moghul Kings of India were Muslim cultures which lacked the simplicity of the Prophet Muhammad's teaching. They were tinged with the personal grandeur and the idea of fame in posterity. In the philosophy of *Kalimah* art and sciences must promote knowledge, goodness and eradicate poverty, ignorance and disease. Abdul Qadir Jilani, Ibn-e-Khaldun, Ibn-e-Sina and Ibn-e-Hayan were the jurist, mathematician, physician and chemist who undertook the task to reveal and uphold the limitless version of the *Kalimah*. The philosophy of life based exclusively on the meanings of the *Kalimah* helped Abdul Qadir Jilani to explore forty different explanations of a certain *Qurānic* verse. Thus he showed the dynamic nature of the *Holy Qurān*.

2. Prayers[35] of a Certain Order to be said Five Times a Day

Prayers are essentially acts of worship and are preceded by ablutions, which involve the washing of hands up to the wrists, rinsing the mouth, running water through the nostrils, washing the face including ears, forehead and chin, arms beyond the elbows, followed by the rubbing of head and ears with wet fingers, and then the right foot and left foot are cleansed up to the ankles. *Bismillah* (in the name of Allah) is recited at the beginning and other formulas are recited during the ablutions.

The five Calls to Prayers which take place before sunrise, soon after midday, three hours after the second, just after sunset, and when twilight disappears, are meaningful and must be said at the right times. An exact number of units called *Raka't* (singular) of all the prayers have certain constant fixed parts of the *Qurān* which are to be recited. For instance, the following is the First Chapter of the *Qurān* called the 'essence of the *Qurān*[36] and is an essential part of every *Raka't*.

> *In the name of Allah, the Beneficent, the Merciful!*
> *Praise be to Allah, Lord of the Worlds, the Beneficent, the Merciful,*
> *Ruler of the Day of Judgment,*
> *Thee alone we worship; Thee alone we ask for help.*
> *Show us the straight path,*
> *The path of those whom Thou has favoured;*
> *Not of those who have earned Thine anger nor of those who go astray.*
> *—Al-Qurān 1: 1-7)*

The other parts of a unit follow certain rules but are left to the discretion of the *Imam* (prayer leader) or the individual concerned if he is alone. The positions of standing, kneeling, squatting and prostrating, again follow the practical steps laid down in any book on Islam. The prayers are concluded by raising both hands together and reciting prescribed Arabic formulas and whatever one wishes to ask of Allah in one's own vernacular.

3. Almsgiving for Charity—*Zakāt*

A share of each Muslim's savings, 2½ per cent, is ordered to go anonymously towards the support of the poor and for the religious education of students in the mosque and the cultural teaching of children (such as happens in Britain in order that they retain their own language).

The principle of *Zakāt* provides the basis for the conception of a Muslim Welfare State. Hoarding of money at the cost of others' suffering is contrary to the Islamic spirit. One example is on record of Muhammad's economist companion, Abu-Zar Ghaffari, who used to stand on the crossroads of Mecca and ask for money from passers-by for the public treasury.

The fact that the interest drawn on 2½ per cent of a Muslim's savings is given away as alms or *Zakāt* might genuinely compel this man to ask the Inland Revenue for the income tax rebate on this part of his earnings. In fact some Muslims in Britain remit the interest on savings in English banks to relatives in Pakistan for distribution to the poor.[38] There is a month of the lunar year named *Zeqaid* when assessment is made for this purpose.

In addition to the obligatory alms, the *Holy Qurān* outlines the following principle of charity, behaviour and attitude:

> *"And do good to parents, kinfolks, orphans, those in need, neighbours who are near, strangers, the companions by your side, the wayfarer you meet and what your right hands possess (servants) for God loves not the arrogant, the vainglorious. . ."*
>
> —*(Al-Qurān 4:36)*

4. Fasting[39] for One Full Lunar Month

Ramadhan is the month during which the Prophet is believed to have received the first revelations from the Angel Gabriel. Muslims fast during it from dawn to dusk daily. Because of the Muslim calendar being a lunar one the fasting month, like other Muslim events, is earlier every year.

The month of *Ramadhan* is very sacred to a Muslim—first, because the revelation to Muhammad was completed in this month; secondly, in the last third of this lunar month there falls a night called *Leilat-ul-Qadar* (the Night of Power) when prayers are met with an exceedingly great kindness by Allah; and, thirdly, the final reckoning with all those who are born or die in the year takes place.

5. Performance of Pilgrimage known as *Hajj* to the Holy Places, especially Mecca and Medina

This should be made at least once in a lifetime, if it can be afforded, to kiss the *Black Meteorite,* the shrine and sanctuary of Allah, which has to be walked around seven times.

The social impact of massive gatherings of people of all classes, colour, education, tongues and cultures in the one place of pilgrimage for some length of time is no less profitable in inculcating the idea of universal brotherhood,[40] than the spiritual doctrine as taught in the *Qurān*. This points to the fact that religion and politics in Islam go hand in hand.

Al-Hajj Malik Al-Shahbaz, better known as Malcolm X (1925-1965 C.E.)

an American negro converted to Islam, has depicted his impression of the pilgrimage he performed in 1964 C.E., in the following words:

> *"During the past 11 days here in the Muslim World, I have eaten from the same plate, drunk from the same glass, and slept in the same bed (or on the same rug). While praying to the same God with fellow-Muslims, whose eyes were the bluest of the blue, whose hair was the blondest of blond, and whose skin was the whitest of the white. And in the words and in the actions and in the deeds of the white Muslim I felt the same sincerity that I felt among the black African Muslims of Nigeria, Sudan and Ghana.*
> *We are truly all the same (brothers) because their belief in one God had removed the 'white' from their minds, the 'white' from their behaviour and the 'white' from their attitude."*
> —*(Malcolm X Pub.   Penguin p453)*

These *Five Pillars of Faith* had Universal appeal and many Muslim states were set up throughout the World. Non-Muslims had nothing to fear because Allah says, *"Let there be no compulsion in religion. . ."* (Al-Qur'ān 2:256). The quotation is well-illustrated by a letter written by a *Nestorian* bishop to his friend during the rule of Caliph Umar:

> *These Tayites (Arabs) to whom God has accorded domination in our days have also become our masters; yet they do not combat at all the Christian religion; on the contrary, they even protect our faith, respect our priests and our saints and make donations to our churches and our convents".*
> —*(Cf. Assemani, Bibl, Orient, III, 2, pXCVI).*

The philosopher Jew, *Jacob Ben Isaac Al-Kindy,* was able to develop Judaism during the reign of the Muslim Caliph *Al-Maamun* (813-833 C.E.).

Innumerable examples of high ranking non-Muslim officials during Muslim rules are found throughout history. There was no coercion as befell the Muslims in Spain.

c.   Early Life, and Social Customs which are binding for Muslims in Britain.

Birth

The overall Muslim population is on the increase throughout the world through birth or conversions. The new-born baby, soon after its birth, listens to the *'Call to Prayer',* the Arabic text and transcription of which is known to almost all Muslims and which is recited to summon Muslims to pray in the mosque instead of the ringing of church-bells. Its words mean:

*"Allah is great; Allah is great: Allah is great: Allah is great. I stand a
witness to the fact that no one is worthy of worship but Allah. I stand
a witness to the fact that no one is worthy of worship but Allah, I also
stand a witness to the fact that Muhammad is the true Prophet of Allah.
I also stand witness to the fact that Muhammad is the true Prophet of
Allah. O brethren in Islam! come to perform the prayers. O brethren
in Islam! come to perform the prayers. O brethren in Islam! come to
achieve salvation. O brethren in Islam! come to achieve salvation.
Allah is great; Allah is great. No one is worthy of worship but Allah".*

Those who wish to be converted take a bath and toilet ablutions and say a
special prayer in the presence of two witnesses. The shaving of a baby's head at
birth is common, a symbolic act to take away the uncleanliness of birth, as well
as to help the hair grow in greater profusion.

Names

Muslim names are often the combination and permutation of the ninety-nine
names of Allah, each meaning a different and principle attribute, and of
Muhammad.

Those teachers concerned with Muslim children might find it convenient for
remembering their names by writing down all the names of an individual and
then grading them according to the usual requirements. It is no good asking
for their 'Christian' names. That will not be understood and is anyway an
anomaly. Their first names are best called common names and can be
supplemented by father's names, dates of birth, and addresses to make them
more certain. There is no such name as 'Abdul'. 'Abd' means servant and 'ul'
is the definite article. These two words are used in conjunction with one of the
attributes of Allah to form a name eg., Abd-ul-Rahman, servant of the
Beneficent (Allah).

Every Muslim has a tribal name based on the name of the area from which
he has come, or from the founder of the clan. This is the equivalent of a
surname. If this could be accepted as such it may solve some of the confusions
which arise from too many *Alis* and *Khans,* and for local authority
departments, and hospital and police records.

For instance a young man may state his name as Abdullah (ie, the servant of
God). This is how he is known in Pakistan. His full name, however, may be
Abdullah Haroon which is a name derived from the famous Muslim Caliph
Haroon or he may be known as *Muhammad Yunus* (the equivalent of *John
Smith).* In this case his father's name can be added, such as *Muhammad
Yunus* son of *Hayat Khan* (whose name again corresponds to *John Smith!)*
The word *Khan* constantly causes confusion. It is not a surname in the

54

Western sense. *Khan* means the head of a tribe, such as *Khan Abdul Ghaffar Khan*. The first is the title, and the latter is part of the name but *not* the surname.

Circumcision

Circumcision is obligatory for a male Muslim child. No age is fixed. It can be at any time before the age of eight. To avoid any subsequent difficulty it can be synchronised with the removal of the baby's umbilical cord scar seven or eight days after the birth. In Britain, if a Muslim doctor is not available there are difficulties as sometimes excessive amounts have been charged (in a few cases £50-£60 for the simple operation). In the Jewish community an over-all charge of £5 is made, as this is not done under the National Health Service. Perhaps this matter can be investigated or Pakistani doctors can perform the simple operation as a community service for their own people, as Jewish doctors have done.

Sacrifice

The *Hajj,* pilgrimage to Mecca, and the *Zakāt*, the tax on one's savings in kind or cash, have definite and concise rules to follow in their execution. Sacrifice of a goat or sheep is again obligatory and is performed by those who can afford it on the eve of *Eid-ul-Adha.* Muslims in this country have been observed performing this duty through help from their dependants in the country of emigration. Anyone who wishes to carry out over here will of course follow the rules of the Local Health Department. Sacrifice of an animal here in Britain is fast becoming the practice of British Muslims.

Money Matters

Whereas insurance of life and property with Government bodies and individual societies is allowed, games of chance and speculation are forbidden.[41] Loans of money are offered to friends without interest. In Pakistan interest from banks is utilised for community development projects or given as alms to the poor but here, for fear that unclaimed interest from money deposited in banks may be donated to schemes opposed to the cause of Islam, interest has been realised even though it is not one of the principles of Muslim faith to accept interest[42] on money.

A loan can be extended to the needy but without interest, to be returned at the borrower's convenience. Investment of wealth in commercial terms is encouraged provided certain principles such as reasonable profits, proper weights[43] and measures and correct terms and conditions in the case of joint enterprises (laid down beforehand) are adhered to.

d. General Habits

Christopher Dawson, writing in *The Dynamics of World History,* has said:

> *'Islam is at once a culture and a religion in which culture can hardly be conceived of as existing apart from religion'.*

Fasting

A fasting Muslim, a slim man who could, clearly, get no slimmer than he actually was, had to explain to an inquisitive British colleague the spiritual benefits gained by fasting. It was, indeed, difficult for him to communicate to the questioner the sharp and subtle improvement acquired in the qualities of tolerance, patience, self-control, resistance to temptation—and even the pleasure experienced in the sacrifice of physical desires. This kind of thing, perhaps, is difficult even for an ascetic to explain clearly without having performed a miracle, and especially in a secular atmosphere where the concept behind fasting is now no longer familiar, and where self discipline is not held at a premium.

On the other hand, one could observe a fasting immigrant child showing signs of listlessness because of his hunger and could, in consequence, conclude that the fasting was having an adverse effect. The question arises, as to whether such children are compelled to fast without knowing the reason. Are the benefits accruing from fasting adequately explained to them? Do immigrant parents themselves know the importance and significance of fasting or even the fundamental injunctions of Islam for that purpose? These are matters of some difficulty in view of the complex nature of the situation and the subject and the relatively poor education of many of the parents who have come to Britain from entirely rural backgrounds. This is more a social and educational problem than a religious one.

Eating

By British Law, it is an offence to keep live chickens in the house. It has, however, been a common practice with Indo-Pakistani settlers though it has declined rapidly. There is, of course, no religious ordinance which would lead people to break the law in this respect. In fact, the meat of any kind of animal slaughtered ritually is available from Indian and Pakistani grocers and butchers and a prompt inquiry from their associations and voluntary organisations can help to stop ill-practices of this kind which are of a behaviouristic rather than religious nature. Much is the result of blind custom rather than intelligent understanding of faith.

Pork and alcoholic drinks are forbidden. Other kinds of meat are the same for Muslims as for Christians, except that there is a difference in the way in which the animals must be killed. The ritual of slaughtering is performed by pronouncing the formula beginning with *Bismillah* (in the name of God) and cutting the throat at one clean stroke on the respiratory tube, the stomach tube and the two big jugular veins and carotid arteries not touching the spinal column, much less severing the head or stunning the animal. The blood should be drained out straight away. There remain such questions as to how Muslims make up their protein deficiencies if they can't get meat which is not ritually killed. It could be, of course, that they forget about such things as 'protein resources' and 'metabolism' and 'protein synthesis'.

Pork Meats
There are strong reasons of hygiene behind the forbidding of pork meat of any kind for human consumption. Zoologically, pigs, rats and man are subject to a lethal disease caused by the trichina worm. Man can pick up trichinosis from eating poorly cooked pork when pigs have eaten infected rats or raw refuse. Cysts in the muscles of the pig, when eaten, can reproduce in the human intestine and the larvae then bore their way into the blood stream—this can eventually cause severe pain, paralysis and even death. One has to remember again the conditions of Arabia at the time of Muhammad and the fact that modern methods of curing pork did not exist and which are even now far from perfect. The intense heat of the desert made such a strict injunction so long-lasting. The Asian systems of medicine—both Muslim *Unani* and Hindu *Ayurvedic*—lay great stress upon the effects of diet, not only to bodily health but to mental personality.

   Among Muslims the pig is regarded as a dirty animal, and the common theory is that human beings take on the tendencies of the foodstuffs that they may eat to extremes. This is noticeable in heavy meat eaters who tend to look gross. Moreover modern research has disclosed that pork meat is more likely to increase the cholesterol deposits in the human arteries and hence influence hypertension more than any other kind of meat.

Alcoholic Drinks
Similarly alcoholic drinks are also forbidden. Gold and silver utensils as food containers and service are again forbidden, because this is like hoarding wealth that could instead go to the poor. Leading a simple life is much stressed by Muhammad who once showed his disapproval when he saw his wife wearing silken embroidered cloth.

The *Holy Qurān*[44] *says:*

   'Forbidden unto you (for food) are carrion, and blood and swine flesh, and that which hath been dedicated unto another than God, and

the strangled, and the dead through beating, and the dead through falling from a height and that which hath been killed by the goring of horns, saving that which ye make lawful by the death stroke of slaughtering and that which hath been immolated into idols, but whoever is forced by hunger, not by will, to sin, for him lo! God is Forgiving, Merciful.'

—(Al-Qurān 16: 15)

Slaughter of animals must be taken in the name of God, *Bismillah*.

Dress[45]

In dress habits women are told to avoid all that is characteristic of the glamour girl. Dress should cover all the parts of the body and should not help to define physical features. In consequence, the anglicising of women so far as dress is concerned is unlikely to occur. Use of cloth made entirely of silk and garments of red colour are discouraged also. This has given rise to the passionate feelings felt by some Pakistani parents concerning the dress for their teenage daughters in schools, for P.E. lessons and in mixed swimming classes.

Hardly a day passes when one doesn't hear or read about a head teacher insisting on English dress from his/her Muslim girl students in the school. Sometimes it results in wasting the useful time of the pupil during this conflict between the teacher and the parents, especially when the latter take the law in their own hands and keep daughters away from school. The Press makes use of such happenings and people interpret this as 'immigrants not conforming to English ways of life'. Issues become confused, and the immigrants are made a sort of scapegoat for political reasons and not educational ones. The workable solution arrived at by a number of Local Education Authorities is the prescription of a uniform different from English dress but suitable for religious observances. In fact in a number of schools the white trousers are worn with tunics or *kameez* made by girls in the needlework classes to a regulation pattern. The Muslim girls have generally been doing P.E. in slacks; separate swimming rotas have been chalked out for girls. At certain places the Muslim girls of secondary age are exempted from swimming if the parents wish it.

Social 'brushing up' in educational reception centres of the new arrivals from overseas or British born children born to immigrant parents residing in socially deprived areas presents a lot of trouble in later school life. This normally consists of training in the use of toilets, road safety, essential requirements of the English school system of education and examinations, school dinners, welfare and health of school children. This is much the same as for the adults. There are problems attached to the delivery of these instructions, especially when the teacher in charge is English and the children have only scanty knowledge of the English language. These problems are however, not acute in the case of the British born. Some of the problems are religious ones, eg, a Muslim child refuses to eat any kind of meat. An idea that has been tried includes some Indian and Pakistani dishes and savouries in the menu. Muslim children would love grilled and chopped meat (except pork) killed ritually and obtained from Muslim shopkeepers in the town.

Greetings and Arabic Formulas
There are many common brief formulas, most of them in Arabic, which a careful Muslim would always say impromptu when alone or in the company of men and women. He would always pronounce *'Bismillah'* (in the name of God) at the beginning of an action and *'Alhamdulillah'* (Praise be to God) at the end. There is a general feeling among those of staunch Faith that each good or bad happening is the Will of God Almighty.

When something is promised in the future a Muslim always says *Inshaallah* (if God be willing) and greets a person by saying *'Assalamu Alaikum'* (Peace be on you). That person in turn greets him: *'Wa-alaikum-us-salaam'* (and peace by on you). Muslims have 'sayings' for various occasions. After sneezing, for instance, they say *'Alhamdulillah'* for having done so successfully and 'sorry' to recompense the disturbance caused to others nearby! One who hears somebody sneezing says *Yar Hamdulillah'*—May God bless you.

The right hand is used for handling good clean jobs and things, while the left is used for dirty jobs. This is also true within the Indian tradition, the left hand being used for personal ablutions.

When entering a house one steps in the door by using the right foot and when leaving it steps out with the left foot.

'Cleanliness is half of the faith' is one of Muhammad's sayings and is observed rigorously. Taking a bath becomes imperative after cohabitation, wet dreams, menses, the time the blood flow stops after child birth and always before large Friday prayers. The process of bath and ablutions involves the removing of traces of dirt or undesirable material on the body. A shower bath is best suited to this purpose rather than lying in one's own dirty water in a bath. Public baths for this reason have always been under much discussion. Paper alone has never been found sufficient in the W.C. Floor toilets without pedestals, with handy approach to a water tap are missed very badly in the West. Some employers of Asian labour have provided these facilities, Bradford Transport Corporation and Heathrow Airport, for example.

It is forbidden to touch the *Qurān* save when in a state of cleanliness.

e. Daily and Funeral Prayers
For daily prayers the requirements needed are any clean piece of land and the

ability to stand with face towards the *Kaaba* in Mecca, clean dress and water for ablutions. The routine five prayers—one in the morning, two in the afternoon, one at sunset and one about two hours after sunset during the day—are obligatory.

In the case of shortage of time, travelling and sickness these prayers can be shortened and even postponed. There are some, however, who would say the prayers at the right time and would never postpone them, and this is an infallible principle.

A Muslim on his death bed pronounces (if he can) the formula: *'There is no deity but God; Muhammad is The Messenger of God'*.

The dead body is given a bath before burial which is preceded by the saying of funeral prayers. This is again governed by certain rules—such as the time, the kind of person leading the prayer, etc. The service can be performed in the absence of the body which might receive burial elsewhere in the world. The dead body is buried in such a way that the grave is dug parallel to Mecca and the face is turned towards it. Lavish spending on graves is not recommended. Muslims resident in Britain often send the corpses back home for burial (the cost being approximately £140) for a number of reasons, though this practice is declining. The religious one (in addition to those based purely on sentiment) is to bury the relative in a big graveyard that is always visited by pious men praying for the dead in the life Hereafter and for forgiveness of sins. This is also the reason why Muslims ask for and are having separate graveyards here in some towns in Britain.

The System of Morality'—Muslim Women

'Respect for Women' is an essential teaching of Islam. 'I advise you to be good to women', Muhammad said to the Muslims many times. *Fatima,* Muhammad's daughter, well known amongst Muslims as the 'Lady of Paradise' and 'Lady of Light', is an embodiment of divine qualities. Besides her, many more saintly women like *Rabia* in the past commanded respect from the masses.

The ancient Babylonians, Assyrians, Persians, Israelites before the time of Moses, Syro-Phonecian races, Athenians and even high caste Brahmins all exercised polygamy. On the other hand Spartan females usually had more than one husband. As society advances monogamy generally comes into practice. The analysis of the position of women folk in Muslim society has been ambiguous and many Christian observers have been bewildered by the social behaviour of Muslim men and women.

The relevant *Qurānic*[46] passages in connection with marriages are: *You may marry two, three or four wives but not more'*, and *'if you cannot deal equitably and justly with all you shall marry only one'*. In the light of these

60

statements plurality of wives is made a controversial point. Nevertheless the word 'equity' to wives (never overlooked by the great Muslim thinkers) has helped the legislator in almost every Muslim state to abolish polygamy except in cases where the first wife is established as barren or that she cannot bring forth a male issue. Due to lack of education and social attitudes it is difficult to establish that male sterility may be the case of infertility also.

Marriage is, according to Islam, a bilateral *social contract.* The parents certainly aid in this by their counsel and their experience in searching or selecting for the right life companion, looking into the whole family background and heredity, but the couple should have the last say in the matter. Illegal practices may exist from region to region and class to class, but the law does not recognise the customs which contravene its provisions and much is being done in Pakistan to eliminate plurality of wives.

Annulment[47] also exists in Muslim law both for husband and wife. The court of justice also possesses the right of separation of the couple on the plaint of the wife if the husband is incapable of fulfilling his conjugal duties, or if he is suffering from a particularly serious sickness of if he disappears for years without leaving a trace.

The fact that a Muslim has more than one wife does not mean he can claim the benefits from the National Insurance Schemes for all the wives although *all* children can receive family allowances. However, this applies in British society for children born out of wedlock. It is generally accepted that the first marriage, the legal one under British law, is the one to which income tax, maintenance laws, social welfare benefits, etc applies. It is the first wife who by law is the 'informant' in case of death of a Muslim husband.

Men who ignore their wives and do not take them into their confidence or who do them an injustice such as beating or confining them if the wives disagree with them or advance an opinion of their own and impose on them what God has not asked, manifest sheer ignorance of the *Qurānic* right and duties of women, and need thorough reorientation of their unhealthy conduct and ideas, but this is a matter of social progress at the village level, rather than religious backwardness.

A Muslim seen with his wife walking three steps behind in the rear either falls in this category, or has a physically unhealthy woman following him!

Romans usually debated whether woman was a 'person' or 'thing' when Muhammad declared 'women are but sisters of men'. Women were not allowed to touch the *Bible* when *Lady Hafsa* at Medina held the *Qurānic* manuscripts in her trust. Time has changed and the Western women now have far more emancipation amongst them than those from the East. Education is the greatest measure in judging what is good and what is bad, but those with little formal education suffer a great impact from the full force of Western films and television. Women cannot be forbidden to watch T.V. The implications and temptations of viewing some programmes can well be imagined.

In view of all this, youth committees should not be surprised if very small numbers of Muslim girls or none at all attend the Civic Youth Clubs. Visits to the clubs, Muslim parents believe, will result in free mixing of girls and boys, leading to immorality. How far they would exercise and impose their views on their children depends on a number of factors such as the education at home, and school and society, etc.

The matter of dress habit again depends on standards of morality and modesty amongst the women of each race. All veiled women are not morally sound, nor bare-legged women immoral and vice versa. The absorption of minority groups sociologically is bound to occur but the thorough study of his religion would tell an individual when he has overstepped his religious principles in observance. The *Shalwar* or *Sari,* for example, is a typical woman's dress, which meets the religious as well as social sanctions. If, however, a *Shalwar* or *Sari* helps a woman to emphasise her body rather than disguise it, then she really needs some other suitable dress.

Birth Control

The issue of birth control which necessarily means the prevention of conception and hence the procreation of children is rather difficult to be answered from the *Qurān* or the traditions of the Prophet which include no precedent of this kind.

In view of infanticide, abortion and other means of getting rid of unwanted children that went on in Arabia before the advent of Islam, the *Qurān*[48] however contains this narration to stop such ill-practices: *'Do not kill your children for fear of poverty. We will provide for them and for you'*. In the circumstances the modern Muslims have adjudged the pros and cons of the issue of birth control using their own discretion.

The general principle has been pointed out in the *Qurān* time and again to weigh the good and evil of a habit and then decide accordingly. While prohibiting the use of alcoholic drinks, for example, the *Qurān*[49] continues to say. . . *'Its sin and evil far outweigh its benefits'*. The factors such as the health of mothers, the effects of heredity, social and economic imbalance, which are some of the dangers in the growth of population of a country, if they are taken into account in detail, seem to be groundless and God's promise, mentioned above, appears to hold good even now and after. Material gains in scientific and technological advancement, the mineral wealth contained in the unexplored lands like the Amazon's basin, Iceland's plains, arable Alaska and the fertile Arctic regions that abound, this vast wealth for human consumption is some of the evidence to support His promise. The immense sources of wealth which the Creator has placed at the disposal of man as a result of his increasing innate habit of exploration meet the demands of our subsistence. All Malthusian fears are unreal and all geographical fetters shattered when one sees the American farmer producing wheat to feed the Indian famine-stricken and OXFAM despatching ship-loads of medicines to the disease-afflicted millions of Africans.

The intellectually sound and theologically well-informed Muslim believes that the sole aim of sexual intercourse is procreative rather than recreative.[50] A prominent Muslim scholar, the late Maulana Seyyed Abul ala Maududi thinks efforts should be geared to explore more land and resources than to inhibit the growth of mankind. Nevertheless the population of Pakistan is growing at a normal pace because of the Family Planning Commission set up by the Government which is working in this field despite the differing views of the people. The loop method is said to have worked well there. Whosoever resists the suggestion on birth control is free to do so and no compulsion is laid down on the family.

The immigrant family after a year of its arrival in this country increases its number of children partly because of long separation and partly because of the small number of the family and the feeling that one more would not be much burden. The Muslim family must be well aware of the religious views on birth control, but presumably would listen to the advice from the Health Department in order to better the children's prospects and their own economic well being as a smaller, more manageable family.

When it has been necessary for a male doctor to carry out a medical examination, the Muslim ladies have often been reluctant to undress. If no lady doctor is available (a great asset to any Local Authority where Asians have settled in some numbers) it will not be a sin according to her religion to expose any part of her body that a male doctor wishes to examine. It may be harmful for her or for the body in her womb, if she is an expectant mother, if a proper medical examination is not made possible because of her unwillingness to take her clothes off. There have been several cases where Pakistani ladies have died in hospital rather than allow themselves to be examined. Again this is a question of social education among people of very orthodox rural background. It should not be forgotten that Islam insists on a great humility to be shown by both Muslim men and women.

Principal Festivals and Timetable for Future Lunar Reckoning
The two principal feasts which occupy a great religious as well as social importance to a Muslim are the breaking of the fast at the end of the month of *Ramadhan* and the sacrifice of the pilgrimage. All kinds of work in the Muslim world cease on these two days, known as *Eid-ul-Fitr* and *Eid-ul-Adha* respectively. Muslim workers will naturally stay away from work if not given an authorised holiday, and some children (as Jewish children already do for

their festivals) will miss school at least in the mornings to attend the large prayers and sermons in the mosque.

Eid-ul-Fitr is held on the first day of the month of *Shawal* and marks the end of the long month of fasting. On this great day of celebration people get up early in the morning, take a bath, say regular morning prayers due every day before sunrise, eat dates or other sweets, and having put on new or clean clothes, set off for the biggest mosque in the town. There they say full prayers which are held soon after sunrise.

Every well-to-do person is meant to give alms to the poor on this day, preferably before the prayers. Detailed standards are laid down for the amount of alms and the eligibility of the receiving persons.

At the end of prayers people usually pronounce *Eid* greeting and embrace one another to fulfil the Prophet's example. They enjoy a sumptuous midday meal and it is a day of happiness. Even in this country the atmosphere of rejoicing is not lost and Eid cards are even sent to, and received from, British friends. In Muslim countries great fairs are held in the villages, young men gather for folk dancing to the insistent rhythms of large drums, children sing songs and the village elders arrange native-style horse races and wrestling.

Eid-ul-Adha is held on the tenth day of the month of *Dhu-rl-Hijjah,* marking the end of the ceremonies of the pilgrimage of the Prophet Ibrahim and the near sacrifice of Ishmael. It is the second great festival of the Muslim calendar which is celebrated to remind Muslims that one should not hesitate to sacrifice anything for the glory of God. Prayers and other rituals are much the same as the earlier *Eid,* but instead of giving alms, the sacrifice of an animal (usually a goat or lamb) is made obligatory. This can be put into practice during any of the three days (excluding night time) beginning with the day of *Eid.*

Details are again set out for the type of animal sacrifice, the disposal, and the distribution of the meat to those in need, etc. This *Eid* also provides a chance for a great gathering of relatives, fun and amusements, and feasts for all.

There are a number of other festivals such as the Prophet Muhammad's Birthday *(Eid-Milad-un-Nabi)* which falls on the twelfth of the month of *Rabi-ul-Awwal,* three months after the Eid of Sacrifice, and *Muhurram.* These are public holidays in Pakistan.

Muharram

Another festival—*Muharram*—commemorates the battle and death of Hussain, the grandson of the Prophet, and the imprisonment of his family during the contest for the succession of the Sixth Caliphate. The tenth day of this month, which is also called *Muharram,* goes even further back in time to the date of the drowning and death of Pharaoh and his army in the river Nile while chasing Prophet Moses and his followers.[51] In gratefulness to this, the Prophet fasted on this day, as do Jews now to commemorate this historic event.

Muhammad also directed Muslims to fast on this day and also on the 9th and 10th of *Muharram*.

Forty years after the death of the Prophet Muhammad during the Caliphate of Yazid, Hussain, his grandson, was killed on the same day. All Muslims know it and every year at the beginning of this month they recite the *Holy Qurān* for the good of his departed soul. The *Shia* sect especially who trace their lineage from Hussains's side of the family, celebrate this day although all Muslims believe in the historical truth of why the battle was fought.

The *Shias* mourn his death for 40 days and meetings are held in the evenings for the first nine days to recall the incidents especially for the benefit of the younger ones. A mourning procession takes place on the tenth day with large *'tazias'* or floats, and with the chanting of religious hymns and ballads. Some of the participants are so moved that tears stream down their faces, and they flagellate their own bodies to 'suffer along with Hussain'. No weddings, TV shows or musical recordings take place around this time. For the English dates of these festivals see the following chart.

The *Hijri* lunar year is 10-11 days shorter than the solar year (354-355 days). Seventy-one days after 1st of the month of *Muharram* (the First new year day) is the Prophet's Day, then after 166 days is followed by the fasting month of *Ramadhan* (29 or 30 days), the end of which is *Eid-ul-Fitr*.

Two hundred and sixty-four days after the Prophet's Day is *Eid-ul-Adha*. This table may be useful for those managements employing predominantly Muslim labour forces because of the difficulty encountered with managements who remain adamant in not giving leave of absence for principal festivals already long-established in other religious communities. On the other hand further notice needs to be given by Muslim associations so that managements know well in advance, and not the day before a Festival, so that the matter can be settled equitably.

Hijri Year	1st Muharram	Prophet's Day	1st Ramadham	Eid-ul-Adha
1397	23 Dec 76	3 March 77	17 August 77	22 Nov 77
1398	12 Dec 77	20 Feb 78	6 August 78	11 Nov 78
1399	1 Dec 78	10 Feb 79	26 July 79	1 Nov 79
1400	20 Nov 79	30 Jan 80	14 July 80	20 Oct 80
1401	9 Nov 80	20 Jan 81	4 July 81	9 Oct 81
1402	31 Oct 81	9 Jan 82	24 June 82	30 Sept 82
1403	20 Oct 82	29 Dec 82	13 June 83	20 Sept 83
1404	9 Oct 83	18 Dec 83	2 June 84	9 Sept 84
1405	28 Sept 84	12 Dec 84	22 May 85	29 Aug 85

1406	17 Sept 85	27 Nov 85	11 May 86	18 Aug 86
1407	7 Sept 86	16 Nov 86	30 April 87	7 Aug 87
1408	26 Aug 87	6 Nov 87	19 April 88	27 July 88
1409	15 Aug 88	24 Oct 88	9 April 89	16 July 89
1410	4 Aug 89	13 Oct 89	29 March 90	5 July 90

A difference of a day on either side of the dates given above can be taken into account subject to the appearance of Moon. All Muslim festivals are subject to the phases of the Moon, and have to take into account the 'siting' of the new Moon as it is called. This in fact means the actual 'sighting' of the new Moon, sometimes impossible in the English climate with low cloud base—therefore Muslim religious leaders confirm this by telephoning religious institutions based in Muslim countries where the new Moon would have been sighted.

The names of the months of the Muslim lunar calendar are as follows:

1. *MUHARRAM*
2. *SAFAR*
3. *RABI-UL-AWWAL*
4. *RABI-UL-THANI*
5. *JAMADI-UL-AWWAL*
6. *JAMADI-UL-THANI*
7. *RAJJAB*
8. *SHAHBAN*
9. *RAMADHAN*
10. *SHAWAL*
11. *DHU-UL-QADAH*
12. *DHU-UL-HIJJAH*

Some Islamic Views

Art

The Prophet did not appreciate portrait drawings but with the times the attitude of the people has changed. However, drawing of the Prophet's profile can even now cause a great row. Muslims have, however, selectively contributed in the field of mosaics and murals and fine works of tracery and floral embellishments. *Al-Hambra* (Spain) and *Taj Mahal* (India) are the living examples of these. This may affect children's attitude to figure drawing. It is best to start a hesitant Muslim child at school with patterns, and floral designs which they are naturally skilled at designing.

Music

The practice of singing without musical instruments is very vague. Only very devout Muslims have abandoned instruments when singing. The children's parents will, of course, object to their children attending religious assembly at school if they think they are being converted to Christianity, and hearing Christian religious hymns.

Religious Education

If some universal truths contained in the *Qurān* and also other Holy Books could be made use of once or twice a week the children from all religious faiths would surely join with English children in morning prayers. In places of dense Muslim concentrations of population, their children attend the local mosques for prayers and learning of their religion and language (Arabic, Urdu or Bengali) during the week and at weekends. The number of hours spent each week at the mosque by typical Muslim children varies from four to six; there are some extreme cases of those who never visit the mosque at all, and on the other hand of those who spend as many as twelve hours there. The education of children in state schools coupled with study in the mosques satisfies the aspiration of Muslim parents.

So long as the child complies with the school regulations and requirements and so long as his parents understand that he will have to compete with native children when trying to achieve his ambitions after school in finding a decent job, no-one can really interfere. After all, English parents decide how many hours their children will spend watching television.

The Muslim child, if he attends the mosque, will have his attitude to Christianity influenced to some extent by his Muslim teachers and his attitudes to his own religion will be influenced by his knowledge of Christianity. These children might appear to by over-worked, but invaluable social education imparted at the mosque has helped the English teacher administratively in many ways. The religious leader of the community can well be a bridge between the school head and Muslim parents in cases of difficulty.

Some teachers in this modern age are of the view that children should not receive any religious instruction. To a Muslim this has dangers—in that the child may become a moralist with his attentions self-centred on humanity, rather than a religionist with attentions centred on God. Muslim parents will always guide their children and the religious instruction in the mosque will always be intensified when the effect of one society upon the other is experienced. Every Muslim parent knows what the Prophet says: *'Every child is born in accord with Divine Nature, it is his parents who make of him a Jew, a Zoroastrian or a Christian'*. This implies that every baby is born a Muslim (unless otherwise directed by its parents) and therefore Muslim parents had a singular duty to reinforce the teachings of Islam. Instead of demanding blind acceptance educated Muslims are beseeched in the *Holy Qurān*[52] to use reasons in understanding the truth and to investigate the natural phenomena in order to realise the word of God in the works of God and to harness natural forces for the realisation of human destiny under the overall direction of the Vice-regency of God.

Iqbal, the philosopher of Islam, visualises the place of religion in life more effectively in his lectures on the *Reconstruction of Religious Thought in Islam* and exhorts to bring about thorough changes in the education of Muslim children in accordance with true religious spirit. 'Experience shows', he maintains, 'that truth revealed through pure reason is incapable of bringing that fire of living conviction which personal revelation alone can bring. That is the reason why pure thought has so little influenced men, while religion has always elevated individuals and transformed whole societies'.

Even in the modern age in connection with the necessity of religious education, he reasoned: 'Religion, which in its higher manifestation is neither dogma, nor priesthood, nor ritual, can alone prepare modern man for the burden of the great responsibility which the advancement of modern science necessarily involves, and restore to him that attitude of faith which makes him capable of winning a personality here and retaining it Hereafter. It is only by raising to a fresh vision of his origin and future his whence and whither that man will eventually triumph over a society motivated by an inhuman competition and a civilisation which has lost its spiritual unity by an inner conflict of religious and political values'.

His concept of Islamic education both in form and content (as is apparent from his poetry) is the one that refuses the acquisition of passive knowledge, but accepts the one that encourages self-knowledge, develops an all-embracing humanism and true international outlook devoid of sectionalism and geographical differences. He aspires towards the type of education that existed in the heyday of Islam, that produced remarkable results. *Briffault,* the famous historian of civilisation, has summed it up like this—'Science is the most momentous contribution of Arab civilisation to the modern world. Nowhere is this, ie, the decisive influence of Islamic culture, so clear and momentous as in the genesis of that power which constitutes the distinctive force of the modern world and the supreme force of its victory—natural science and the scientific spirit'.

Even if the progress in scientific and technological fields in the Islamic states is at a low ebb after the early centuries of leading the world, yet overall education is thoroughly imbibed at the religious level. This has relevance for religious education in British Schools where a preponderance of Asians attend a primary school (sometimes well over 50 per cent). There is a pressing need for religious education to cater for a multi-religious society. Even in the West, students are seeking beyond narrow religious boundaries and are looking outward to the good in all the world's faiths.

The biggest danger in excessive 'integration' is that children grow up not knowing about their own religion and history, thinking themselves 'English' but when they leave school disillusionment sets in and they are neither English nor Pakistani, neither Christian nor Muslim, rootless like the Negro youths in USA cities.

But theory is one thing, practice another. There are those Muslims who outwardly seem not to be practising the tenets of their faith, but who in the final analysis would stand by their faith.

A drinking Muslim once had an argument with a non-Muslim who abused him and his religion. This is where those dealing with the issue and trying to bring reconciliation between the various elements of society will have to remember that a *non-practising Muslim* (one who drinks alcohol, for instance) is unrepresentative of the integrity and true honour of the Muslim faith. Religious faith in a cross-section of society is blind, for a very small proportion of the world's populace actually think out the beliefs handed down to it by ancestors. Those who do ponder on such matters find them not at all easy to grasp. Islamic ideology has always laid great stress on reasoning out of natural phenomena, investigation of surroundings and harnessing[53] of natural forces for human good.

The Religious Upbringing of Muslim children at home, in the Mosque, at school in the Muslim World, and in Britain*

Introduction

The average English man who comes to know of the existence of a number of Muslim mosques at places of Muslim concentration might well wonder what is going on within. Primarily these, as in their native countries, are places of worship for all, and especially for the religious instruction of children. The mosques in England, however, have taken on extra responsibility of providing social education and instruction in language and religious essentials. The main reason for this is that Muslim children attending English schools receive little education in Islamic theology, whereas in schools such as in Pakistan this is part of their school curriculum and syllabus, and the timetable is built around the prayers. The day starts with prayers (which has a special relevance to education), or with national songs in primary and secondary schools.

Home

From birth, Muslim children grow up at home with the Muslim Faith and traditions in practice. If not all, at least one member of the family is seen praying five times a day. The children are there to hear some calls to prayers daily and they would notice the difference in the construction of their own homes and the mosque. Thus environmental influence alone may help them to learn a great deal about their Faith.

The daily work begins with early morning prayers preceded by washing or ablutions loud recitation of the *Holy Qurān* by female family members,

---

*This section is reproduced from *Religion in the Multi-Faith School,* a publication of the Yorkshire Committee for Community Relations.

followed by breakfast. The children visit the mosque to learn from the *Imam,* the religious leader. They have ample opportunities to watch the common ceremonies and customs attendant at the time of birth, circumcision, marriage, and death; and festivals of fasting, *Eid-ul-Fitr, Eid-ul-Adha,* and *Eid-Milad-un-Nabi* (the Prophet's Day). The extent of their activities in these events is determined by their age. Whilst the children are away at school, mother looks after the household duties and the father sets off to the farm reciting the *Holy Qurān* verbally. Every home has 2-3 copies of the *Qurān,* which is handled with great respect when carried to the mosques and back home.

All kinds of work stop at noon during summer and in the early afternoon during winter. The early and late afternoon, evening and late evening prayers are short periods of worship for both men and women. Preferably men go to the mosque for their prayers. Older children also attend. *Lota* (a utensil for ablutions), rosaries, and prayer-carpets are ubiquitous and offered as presents to young ones and family friends.

The Mosque

The *Imam* in the mosque does not finish his work until an hour after the early morning prayers. The boys and girls come to the mosque before they eat their breakfast and memorise the Arabic text (and its meanings) of the prayers at the age of 4-6. After this age they read the *Holy Qurān.* The visits to the mosque continue until a child can say the prayers and read the *Qurān.* Some may embark upon learning it by heart. The process entails a good deal of skill and labour and is conducted in special schools called *"Madrissahs".*

The older boys and girls attend to the cleanliness of the younger ones and help the *Imam* in teaching them. The *Imam* reports to the parents on matters concerning progress and discipline. In his time between the prayers he looks after his own family and attends to the religious ceremonies for all in the area. Usually, he invites the learned men who lecture on Muslim history, law and doctrines. The *Qaris* (those who can chant the *Qurān* sweetly) recite the *Qurānic* verses and also sing Urdu-Panjabi poems which cover the reappraisal of the Prophet Muhammad's and his followers' lives. Such events last overnight and even for days especially during the fasting month of *Ramadhan.* The young boys also participate in singing and recitation.

Schools

In schools, a compulsory subject of Islamic Studies is introduced for all until entering a degree course at 16. The vastly comprehensive syllabuses available from the directorate of education and various universities in Pakistan consist of Islamic history, Muslim theology, and worship. Study during the early school days is made easy because of the visits to the mosque.

In the sixth year of their school life children learn to speak English and Persian (or Arabic) as second languages just as French or German is taught to English children. As the language improves, books including extracts from the famous Muslim writers such as RUMI, SAADI, AL-HARIRI, and UMAR KHAYYAM are introduced. The older children enjoy the extracts from SHAIKH SAADI SHIRAZI'S (d. 1292 A.D.) *GULISTAN (The Rose Garden) and BUSTAN (The Orchard),* because of their sufic subtleties explained through short stories. Both these books, which are regarded as masterpieces of Persian literature, are available in English and other major languages.

The moral stories of SAADI (of the type given below) and others are written in Urdu or Persian but are often of no use to Muslim children educated in Britain who may only have a limited knowledge of Urdu script however hard they try at the mosque and may not find time in their later industrial life to read the difficult translations in English.

> *"A dog bit the foot of a Bedouin with such fury that poison dripped from its teeth and the pain at night was so great that sleep could not comfort him. Now in his household he had a little daughter who upbraided him and was very angry. 'Did you too not have teeth?' she asked. The unhappy man ceased his wailing and said, laughing: 'My darling little mother, even though I had the power and a spear too, yet it would revolt me to use my own jaws and teeth. It would be impossible for me to apply my teeth to a dog's leg even if a sword were held at my head'. The nature of dogs is evil, but man cannot (in defence) act like a dog".*
>
> —*(adopted from REUBEN LEVY'S translation)*

The ensuing collection of Muslim religious stories are true historical events. It is becoming increasingly obvious that there is a definite need for a good selection of moral stories from Islamic literature for both teachers and pupils.

The British Mosques

The mosques in England partly resemble the ones of the Islamic countries in the 11th Century, when these institutes of learning were responsible for the social, cultural, religious, scientific, and artistic education of the people at that time.

With a number of objectives in mind Muslim parents send their children to the mosque regularly during the evenings and during the day over the weekend. The average attendance per week for all age groups, after the age of four, is three to four hours, but there are those who do not put in an attendance at all and others who put in as much as ten to thirteen hours per week.

Incidentally, the mosques in different towns and cities, ie, London, Birmingham, Glasgow, Bradford and Huddersfield, do not conform with the customary architectural design—they are often just terrace houses with the inner walls removed—there are no minarets or tombs but arrangements are made for ritual ablutions and direction of prayers towards the Holy City of Mecca.

The governing body, usually called the Mosque Committee, employs a religious leader well conversant with the languages of the East, whose duties are many and manifold. He teaches the children the rudiments of language and religion, conducts prayers five times a day, and funeral prayers when the occasion demands.

Social Teachings

A function that has only recently been introduced into a number of mosques is the teaching to the children of certain sections of the Highway Code; this has been brought about by the increasing concern of the Road Safety Departments of the Borough Police and by the Welfare Department of the Local Education Authorities at the alarming rise in road accidents to immigrant children, especially those between the age of three and five years. To assist the New Commonwealth Communities to become road safety conscious a section of the Highway Code has been translated into Urdu—the *lingua franca* of the majority of settlers from India and Pakistan—and presented in the form of a booklet (Reference: Bradford and West Yorkshire Constabularies).

The children, themselves, are bridging the gap between the Eastern and Western world; they are absorbing things from both the mosque and the state school and in this way are helping their parents to broaden their outlook on life in a changing situation. The religious leaders of some of the Mosques have made it a permanent feature of their sermons to the children to ask their parents to attend local English classes for adults. In this way they prove very helpful to the Further Education Departments in their endeavour to help the non-English speaking settlers. Once the English classes have begun, the religious leaders' sermons are geared to maintain interest in the classes and uphold their motives. Still another function of the mosque is to introduce the cross-section of the Muslims attending the large Friday afternoon prayers to such current events as *'The Year for Racial Harmony'*, *'Human Rights Charters'*, *International Year of the Child*, and *'Relationship between Muslims and Christians'* in different towns.

Publications

Some mosques are producing printed matter varying from small occasional papers and bulletins to voluminous monthly magazines, purely on Islam in all its facets and different prospectives. The Shah Jahan Mosque at Woking

Surrey, the oldest in this country, is publishing *"The Islamic Review"*—an English monthly in its 80th year of publication. A number of other mosques up and down the country are contemplating producing literature in both English and Urdu to help parents to teach their children the basic tenets of Islam from the modernist's point of view. The Union of Muslim Organisation's, which has for some time been set up in London, is looking into the needs of the English speaking children, and has, in fact, produced a few useful primers in English. The Union has also set up a National Muslim Education Council for this purpose.

The Imam

The *Imam* can often be of great help to the Head Teachers of schools with a high proportion of minority children on roll, by explaining the principle of ritual slaughtering of animals and the reasons why children refuse to eat pork at school. To avoid confusion the pre-school children are being taught at the mosque what to eat and what to refuse. Sometimes the difficulties that arise with regard to dress and dietetic customs are caused by confusion over what is religious and what is non-religious and purely a social habit.

With both day and evening study it might appear that these children are being grossly overworked but the fact remains that the education they receive in the mosque covers all the aspects of social education which an English teacher might find great difficulty in imparting to the Muslim child.

Example of the Mosque Teaching

There are certain aspects of Islam which are of intense interest for the Muslim children alone. The following extract, for example, is from the authentic collections of the sayings of the Prophet Muhammad (may Allah bless him) by AL-TIRMIDHI (d. 888 A.D.) and ABU DAUD (d. 888 A.D.), the famous reporters, and is often repeated and common narration for Muslim children in the Mosque to bring home certain lessons.

Saad (may Allah bless him) was one of the Prophet Muhammad's companions. Once the Prophet visited him. He stood by the side of the door and greeted him saying, *"Assalamu Alaikum"*, meaning peace be on you. Saad replied rather quietly, *"Wa-Alaikum-Salam"*, meaning and peace be on you. Qais (may Allah bless him), one of Saad's sons remarked that the Holy Prophet was coming and would he please call him in. Saad said to him, "Be quiet, let him greet us again. The Prophet's well wishing brings a lot of wealth. The more he wishes the better it is".

The Prophet was standing at the door and he greeted Saad for a second time. Again Saad replied only quietly. The Prophet greeted him again but did not hear Saad's soft reply. Having greeted the man three times without receiving any reply the Prophet turned away and was about to go when Saad ran to him and said, "May Allah help me to sacrifice my life for you, the fountainhead of Islam. I heard all your *Salams* (blessings). But I craved for more blessings from you. Is it not good fortune that you, the exalted Prophet of Allah, pray for peace for us? O Prophet! The human beings do strange things for love and this gesture of mine was in love for you. Please forgive me for this rudeness and walk in and bless us with your presence".

The Prophet walked in. It was one of the hot days of summer. Saad prepared a bath for the Prophet. After his bath he put on a saffron coloured sheet, which his host had offered him, and prayed to Allah for his blessings for the family.

Saad brought some food, which the Prophet ate. After a short while when the Prophet asked Saad's permission to go he offered him his horse to ride. He put a red cloth on the back of the horse and ordered Qais to go with the Prophet. Qais walked alongside the riding Prophet. They had gone off only a little when the Prophet asked him to sit on the horse. When Qais would not agree the Prophet told him to go back home. Qais said *salam* to the Prophet and went away,

The story brings home such points as that greetings hold the status of a prayer and is meaningful blessing which has now become a part of Islamic civilisation. The answer to the greeting holds equal importance. The simple permission to enter a house may be refused if the greeting is not given. If greeting three times does not bring any reply then entering a house is not allowed. Returning home happily is the only alternative. People should not stand right in the middle of the doorway whilst asking permission to enter. Peeping inside is strictly forbidden. Hospitality of the guest is a sacred task and walking a few steps with a departing guest is a part of the farewell gesture. The host comes back only when the guest tells him to do so. Offer transport if you have any. Don't be cross if the host does some funny thing out of respect, but instead appreciate it. Disclose your name when asked by the people inside the house. Love is enhanced by short interludes of absence in your visits.

Such are the stories which one comes across quite frequently in the Islamic text books in use in Pakistani state schools catering for the R.E. needs of all age groups. They are of varying length and depth obtained from the sayings of the Prophet and the biographies of the Rashidin Caliphs and the just kings/Caliphs of other dynasties such as Umar bin Abdul Aziz, Haroon al-Rashid, Mahmud Ghaznavi, Qutab-ud-Din, and Aurangzeb Alamgir. Their lives are similar to that of the Prophet, and their practices are highlighted by narrating stories to the students in the classroom. The events devoid of inter-religious encounters can be usefully incorporated in books on world religions without giving offence to any other religious denomination.

Exclusive Muslim Teaching

Experience has shown that the study of the Islamic theology devised for all ages of school children throughout the Muslim world also includes incidents where superiority of the Muslim faith is emphasised. In the mosque everybody, indiscriminate of age, listens to sermons voicing both Islamic orientated and egalitarian views particularly on Fridays. People will listen to these stories again and again, thus the meanings become clearer each time.

One example of the superiority of the miraculous powers of the Prophet Muhammad relates how Abu Bakr, the first Caliph of Islam, reported that when he and the Prophet Muhammad (may Allah bless him) were forced to leave Mecca, 'a man named Saraqa bin Malik chased us. I could see that he was closing upon us so I said to the Prophet, "Now we are, indeed, caught by this person." The Prophet replied, "Do not worry, Allah is with us." Then he prayed and to our amazement we saw Saraqa's horse sink down into the hard earth till only its body and head were above ground and Saraqa's legs were stuck fast. Saraqa called out, "I know that you have both prayed for my misfortune. Now pray that I may get out again. In return, I promise that I will stop all those who are out searching for you". The Prophet returned to his prayers and soon Saraqa was a free man'. Saraqa kept his word and turned away all those who were chasing the Prophet and his companions.

The events may be compared with the sinking of Qaroon and his palace. It is reported that Qaroon made the Prophet Moses' (may Allah bless him) life hell on earth. But as he was the Prophet's cousin the Prophet always forgave him.

When the Prophet had the Divine Call to ask people to pay *"Zakāt"* (the giving of compulsory alms to the poor) he demanded that Qaroon should pay *Zakāt* if not at the standard rate of 2.5% of the savings at least one Dirham out of one thousand. Qaroon estimated that even at the reduced rate he would have to pay to the poor a huge sum of money. He thought of a plan to turn the Israelites against Moses.

All the same Qaroon bribed a bad woman to accuse the Prophet of immoral relations with her.

It was the day of Eid. Before the Eid prayers the Prophet Moses preached a sermon which prescribed the just punishment of thieves and adulterers. The latter was to be stoned to death. Qaroon interrupted and shouted, "What if you yourself have committed adultery?" The Prophet answered that he should be punished likewise. At this Qaroon announced that the Prophet had committed adultery with an Israelite woman.

The Prophet called for the woman who swore under oath that Qaroon bribed her to accuse him of this sin. Hearing this, the Prophet fell on to his knees and prayed to God to decide Qaroon's punishment. His prayers were met and a revelation commanded him that earth was made subservient to Moses in order to punish Qaroon. The Prophet Moses said, "O, Earth! catch hold of Qaroon." Qaroon slowly sank into the earth up to his knees. At the second command he was swallowed up to his waist, at the third up to his neck until he sank completely.

As soon as the earth started swallowing Qaroon, he repeatedly asked the Prophet for his mercy, but he would not forgive him. Allah, the Compassionate and Merciful, told Moses that had Qaroon asked Him for mercy only once he would have been forgiven.

After this happening the Israelites accused Moses of taking Qaroon's wealth. He became angry and in a rage ordered the earth to swallow Qaroon's palace and wealth. Thus everything sank.

Although the events are similar yet the Prophet Muhammad showed mercy and forgave the accused. Not only that, Saraqa was given a certificate of peace and told that he would have good fortune later in life.

REFERENCES

All references are to the *Holy Qurān* translated by Muhammad Marmaduke Pickthall—Allen and Unwin.

1. 3:19
2. 22:78
3. 55:34
4. 6:12
5. 36:38, 40
6. 112:1-4
7. 5:3
8. 2:142-3
9. 18:62-82
10. 17:1
11. 112:1-4
12. 17:2, 77; 21:78-82; 19:27-36; 2:11-36
13. 37:101-108
14. 42:13
15. 41-43
16. 13:30, 37
17. 2:213; 10:19; 21:92
18. 3:20; 42:15
19. 5:48
20. 2:2-3
21. 49:30, 13
22. 33:21; 68:4 96:1-5
23. 26:3 28:46; 2:190
24. 18:110
25. 76:80
26. 57:1-3
27. 2:219
28. 35:24
29. 3:84
30. 2:272; 3:130
31. 4:9, 135, 181-183
32. 5:3-9
33. 4:92
34. 17:32; 24:2: 4:25
35. 4:103
36. 1:1-5
37. 22:41
38. 9:60
39. 2:183
40. 4:1
41. 2:219
42. 2:272; 3:130
43. 4:92
44. 16:115
45. 24:30, 31; 33:33, 35, 59, 55
46. 4:3, 28, 129
47. 4:34, 35, 130; 2:228, 234, 235; 33:49; 65:4
48. 17:31
49. 2:219
50. 2:222-223
51. 17:101-106; 26:51; 67
52. 3:189-191; 13:1-4; 3:18-28
53. 13:11

BIBLIOGRAPHY

Suggestions for further reading. Those books, published abroad, can sometimes be ordered from Pakistani bookshops in Britain.

Islam, Alfred Guillaume; Penguin Book.

The Eternal Message of Mohammad, Abdul Rahman Azam; A Mentor Book.

Introduction to Islam, Publication of Centre Cultural Islamique; Paris.

The Saint of Jilan (Ghaus-ul-Azam), S A Salik; Ashraf Press, Lahore.

Anthology of Islamic Literature, James Kritzeck; Penguin Book.

The Darwishes or Oriental Spiritualism, J P Brown; Oxford, 1927.

The Spirit of Islam, Syed Amir Ali; University Paperback, Methuen, London.

Sufism—An Account of the Mystics of Islam, A J Arberry; George Allen and Unwin Ltd.

Muslim Institution (Translation from the French by John P Macgregor), Maurice Gaudefroy Demombynes: George Allen and Unwin Ltd.

Three Major Problems Confronting the World of Islam, Dr Said Ramadan; Islamic Centre, Geneva.

The Meaning of the Glorious Quran, M M Pickthall; London, 1930.

Tafheem-ul-Quran (Translation of the Holy Quran), Maulana Seyyed Abulala-Maududi; Lahore.

Sahih Muslim, translated by Abdul Hamid; Ashraf Press, Lahore.

The Reconstruction of Religious Thoughts in Islam, Dr Sir Muhammad Iqbal; Lahore.

Women in Islam, Muhammad Mazhar-ud-Din Siddiqui, Lahore.

Islam in Theory and Practice, Maryam Jameelah (formerly Margaret Marcus of New York); Lahore.

Islam and Modernism, Maryam Jameelah; Lahore.

Iqbal, His Art and Thought, Syed Abdul Vahid; John Murray, London.

Kitab-ul-Amal-bis-Sunnate—Tarteeb Sharif (The Holy Succession), Barkat Ali, *Dar-ul-Ehsan,* Faisalabad, Pakistan.

The Benefactor, Fakir Seyyed Waheed-ud-Din; Karachi.

Towards Understanding Islam, Seyyed Abul-ala-Maududi; Lahore, 1970.

Letters on Islam, Muhammad Fadhal Jamali; OUP 1965.

The Sacred Journey, Ahmad Kamal; George Allen and Unwin Ltd, 1964.

The Life of Muhammad, by Ibn Ishaq—translated by A Guillaume; OUP, 1955.

The Legacy of Islam, Ed, Sir Thomas Arnold and A Guillaume, OUP, 1931

Thinking about Islam, John B Taylor, Lutterworth Educational, 1971.

Muhammad and the Islamic Tradition, Emily Dermingham; Longmans, 1958.

The Manners and Customs of the Modern Egyptian, E W Lane; Everyman's Library (Dent).

Ideals and Realities of Islam, Seyyed Hossein Nasr; George Allen and Unwin Ltd, 1966.

The Way of the Muslim (Third Edition), Dr M Iqbal; Hulton Educational Publications Ltd, 1973.

The Muslim Community—Islam from Within, Dr M Iqbal; Article in *Understanding some other Religions,* Journal (No 23) of Christian Brethren Research Fellowship; Bristol, 1972.

Religion in the Multi-Faith School, Ed. W O Cole, YCCR, Leeds, 1973.

Islamic Education and Single Sex Schools, Dr M Iqbal; Union of Muslim Organisations of the UK and Eire, London, June 1975.

The Guiding Crescent (Second Edition—Enlarged), Dr M Iqbal, *Dar-ul-Ehsan Publications,* Huddersfield, 1977.

Understanding Your Muslim Neighbour, Dr and Mrs M Iqbal, Lutterworth Press, Guildford, Surrey, 1976.

Salat-ul-Juma't-ul-Mubarik—Friday Congregational Prayers, Barkat Ali, *Dar-ul-Ehsam Publications,* Huddersfield, 1975.

Hajja't-ul-Wida'—The Farewell Hajji, Barkat Ali; *Dar-ul-Ehsan Publications,* Huddersfield, 1975.

Islam, its Meaning and Message, Ed. K. Ahmad, Islamic Council of Europe, London, 1975.

Guidelines and Syllabus on Islamic Education, Education Committee; Union of Muslim Organisations of UK and Eire, London, 1976.

Teaching in the Multi-Cultural School, Ed. James Lynch, Ward Lock Educational, London, 1981.

The Prophets—I, Dr. Syed Ali Ashraf, Hoddert Stoughton, Sevenoaks, 1980.

Drawing on Islam for School Curriculum—An Art in Teaching in the Multi-Cultural School—Dr M Iqbal, Wardlock Educational, London, 1981.

SIKHISM

by *Sardar* Arjan Kirpal Singh

Those Sikhs, who have been initiated through the 'Sikh Initiation' ceremony, become 'KHALSA'. Therefore, 'SIKH' and 'KHALSA' are inter-changeable nomenclatures.

Sikhs meet the West
Initially, it was through the diverse written accounts of the 17th, 18th and 19th Century European travellers, traders, merchant adventurers, missionaries, emissaries, accredited crown political agents at the Mughal Courts, army officers, freelance Chroniclers, amongst others, that the West became aware of the existence of the Sikh people and their homeland—Panjab, the land of Five Rivers, geographically situated in the North-Western part of the Indian sub-Continent, and, because of its strategic location, historically destined to serve as an arena for battling cultures, civilisations, races, mighty armies and religions.

A discursive survey of the early source material, relating to the Sikh/Khalsa, mainly in the English, French and Persian languages, is amply indicative, at times in vivid and moving detail, of the physical and moral aspects of Sikh/Khalsa courage and character, and the defiant spirit of independence. The focussed portrayal of these traits is directly connected with the heroic stand the Sikhs' assumed while combating the evils of bigotry, and the social and cultural oppression excesses of some of the past political masters of India. Therefore taking into account the context and nature of the political and religious climate, the Sikh/Khalsa had to pay a high price for the vindication of their convictions, values and ideals.

What seems to have impressed these European observers was the astonishing physical courage displayed by Sikh/Khalsa in the face of torture and opression; their stoic indifference to death in the noblest traditions of martyrdom.

Ideologically every Sikh/Khalsa is a committed soldier of God, a crusader to uphold righteousness and a challenger and declared destroyer of evil. Imbued with such zeal and sense of mission, innumerable Sikh/Khalsa unhesitatingly wore the crown of martyrdom, while staunchly defending the cherished ideals of Universal freedom of religion and worship, liberty and human rights, the reality of a tolerant, pluralistic society.

In the aftermath of the annexation of the sovereign Sikh/Khalsa kingdom to the British India in 1848 A.D. the British quickly realised and began appreciating the sterling qualities of the Sikh/Khalsa character, martial background and experience. It was clearly recognised by the British that providing the goodwill and co-operation of the Sikh/Khalsa could be won, it would mean valued loyal friends and totally dependable soldiery. Eventually, the Sikh/Khalsa featured prominently in the Indian defence forces during the British 'Raj'. So there grew up a close British-Sikh/Khalsa bond. However, it was the outbreak of the First and Second World Wars that brought about deployment of the Sikh/Khalsa armies in various theatres of action in Europe and North Africa,thus providing the first introduction of the Sikh/Khalsa in significant numbers, to the West. Some Sikh/Khalsa army units were stationed in the U.K. as well. It is a matter of proud record that the Sikh/Khalsa soldiers won an impressive number of the 'Victoria Crosses'—representing the highest military honour for proven valour.

The cessation of the Second World War was closely followed by the fateful partition of the Indian sub-Continent into two independant states. As a consequence, the fortunes, of the Sikh/Khalsa nation was adversely affected. A major segment of Sikh/Khalsa people were uprooted. In the wake of this holocaust, the Sikh/Khalsa understandably turned to their friends i.e. the British. Consequently, it was during the 1950's that there occurred an exodus of the Sikh/Khalsa from India, mainly bound for Britain, Canada and the U.S.A.

Numerically, the total Sikh/Khalsa population amounts to over twelve million. While nine million Sikhs/Khalsa are domiciled in the Panjab and other parts of India, the remaining three million live in virtually all parts of the globe.

There are over two hundred thousand Sikh/Khalsa living in various regions of the United Kingdom. Outside India, this probably represents the largest concentration of the Sikhs/Khalsa in any one country. Besides the U.K. the other countries with notable Sikh/Khalsa presence are Canada, U.S.A., Fiji Islands, New Zealand, Australia, East Africa and several countries in the Far East.

Thus, owing to a combination of historical circumstance, the Sikh/Khalsa, from a position of relative obscurity, have now emerged on the international scene as a familiar sight, particularly in the West. It is no longer an uncommon experience to meet the Sikh/Khalsa working in various professions and sectors of the advanced industrial societies, e.g. medical, engineering, legal, education, scientific, industrial and commercial. Nevertheless, the Sikh/Khalsa are still associated with their traditional occupations such as farmers, agriculturists, sportsmen, athletes, policemen but above all SOLDIERS.

However, my thesis is that in order to appreciate the true character, disposition, and conduct of the Sikh/Khalsa, it is necessary to probe deeper and discover its primal power and strength.

Such a preliminary investigation prompts five key questions and the suggested answers hopefully should clarify the issue:—

1. Who or what is a SIKH/KHALSA ?

Essentially a Sikh/Khalsa is a deeply religious person and his/her unswerving devotion to the spiritual commitments, as embodied in the Sikh Way of Life—Sikhism—is unquestionably TOTAL. For the Sikh/Khalsa his/her religion constitutes the primary, motivating, element in every aspect of his/her spiritual and secular life, both at individual and societal level.

2. What is the source of the celebrated Sikh/Khalsa fortitude, tenacity and courage ?

The key to this answer lies exclusively in the nature, structure and divine strength of the Sikh religion itself, as bequeathed to the Sikh/Khalsa by the Ten Sikh Gurus—-Guru Nanak to Guru Gobind Singh and Guru Granth Sahib—the Sacred Sikh Scriptures.

In short, it is impossible to understand and know a Sikh/Khalsa, in a meaningful sense, without some knowledge about his/her religious and spiritual heritage.

3. What is the connotative significance of the concept of 'soldiership' for the Sikh/Khalsa ?

The nature and spirit of the concept of soldiership is avowedly professed by the Sikh/Khalsa can be categorically stated thus: that, he/she humbly acknowledges himself/herself to be a soldier of the Almighty, Timeless God and constantly remains in total submission to God's Will or Command. A Sikh/Khalsa considers himself to be a crusader, who is everready to engage in war against evil and defend and uphold righteousness. It is his/her religious duty to fight against oppression and, if need be, die fighting.

4. What is the relationship of the Sikh/Khalsa to Society and the World ?

The Sikh/Khalsa is acutely conscious of his/her personal, family, community and civic obligations, and as obligatory part of religious discipline, he/she must dutifully carry out the secular duties as well. It is through the service and practice of expressive care of humanity that a Sikh/Khalsa effectively substantiates true love for God. In the world of human affairs the personal qualities of Love and disinterested Service must engage him/her, Truthfulness and Righteous conduct must occupy him/her, and Compassion and Mercy must move him/her.

5. Is there a complement to the soldierly character of Sikh/Khalsa ?

The question has logically brought us to the high point of this enquiry. The answer is a resounding, YES. Indeed, the perfect complement counterpart of the soldierly spirit is of SAINTLINESS.

First and foremost, the Sikh/Khalsa is a humble servant and creature of God—a Saint—and the exclusive source from which he derives his strength, vitality and courage, that characterise him as a noble soldier, is emphatically located in this religious inheritance. Therefore, the inner spiritual essence takes precedence and duly determines the attributes of the Saint-Soldier. It is averred that the Sikh/Khalsa is a Saint-Soldier, and his total being is composed in the unique harmonization of these dual facets. It is seldom realised by Westerners and others that the Sikh Gurus evolved and presented a new model of Man and Society.

Finally, I will restate the cardinal proposition that the integral aspects of the inherent bipolar ideal of the Sikh/Khalsa religion and Way of Life ultimately finds its expression in the Saint-Soldier model of Man—a simultaneous embodiment of both, the Holy and Earthly.

Sikhism and its emergent evolution

The word 'Sikh' is the Panjabised version of the classical Sanskrit classical expression 'shishyu' literally meaning a 'Seeker', or 'Aspirer'. 'SIKHISM', in transliteration, denotes 'Seekerism' or 'Followership' of the 'ONE Absolute Supreme God' and the ideal of the universal Love and Spiritual Fellowship of Humankind.

There are distinctive and readily identifiable Sikh/Khalsa religious, ethical, and cultural, perspectives, which were founded, developed, and given shape by the Ten Founder Sikh Gurus—Guru Nanak to Guru Gobind Singh,—over an historical time-span of 239 years. The Guru Granth Sahib—The Sacred Scriptures of the Sikhs—embodies and symbolically personifies the primal source and ultimately spiritual repository of the 'GURMAT'—'Divine Wisdom'—and the code of the Sikh/Khalsa Way of Life.

'Guru Period' in Sikh history

Historically, the 'Guru Period' signifies the time dimension, April, 1469 to October, 1708, during which its nascent Sikhism, its ideals and institutions were evolved and tenderly nurtured to maturity under the personal care, concern and guidance of the Ten Sikh Gurus.

The history of the Sikh Religion appropriately commences with the corporeal advent of its First Founder Guru, Nanak, in April, 1469, at a village called 'Talwandi'—now known as 'Nankana', deservedly named after its celebrated and enlightened son 'Nanak', the Guru, divinely destined to become the 'Master Architect' of the Sikhism—situated about forty miles from Lahore, in the medieval Panjab. Guru Nanak was born of the traditional Hindu parents of the 'Kshatriya' caste. His father was a person of substance, occupying the well respected and influential governmental position of Land Revenue Officer.

The Biographical accounts dealing with Guru Nanak's early life describe him as a precocious, thoughtful, inquisitive and quiet child. At the age of seven years he was sent to the village school, where he received instruction in the elements of the Hindu religion and Sanskrit and Devanagri languages. A year later he was enrolled under the tutorship of a Muslim teacher at the local mosque, where he mastered the rudiments of the Arabic and Persian languages, accountancy and other subjects. Guru Nanak's schooling was marked by intellectual brilliance and the depth of his thought and the searching questions that he frequently posed baffled his Hindui and Muslim teachers.

As he grew up, his preoccupation with matters of the human spirit and God intensified, and he progressively developed a meditative and inquiring frame of mind. He attempted to unravel the mysteries of the Nature in order to make sense of the world around him. He responded sensitively to the seasonal flows and changing landscape of the Panjab, from the hot, dusty summers, to the lush green and hot monsoon north, and the invigorating cold of the winter.

During his formative years, Guru Nanak displayed a shrewd and perceptive awareness of prevailing religious, political, social and cultural affairs. The existence of a variety of religions and demonimational Orders, geared to a wide range of ritual, ceremonialism and modes of worship, also with a supportive network of social relations, exerted a profound impact on his impressionable and receptive mind. However, above all else, the young Guru Nanak had an insatiable yearning for spiritual perfectibility. He possessed a defiantly independent spirit and effulgent piety as it appropriately confirmed by the following events:

At the age of nine years, Guru Nanak was asked by the family Pandit or Brahmin Hindu priest, to undergo the ceremony of wearing the sacred thread, 'yagypwit' or 'Janeu', as was traditionally enjoined upon all high caste Hindus by the authority of the 'Vedas'—the Hindu scriptures. Characteristically, Guru Nanak enquired of the Pandit the explanation and reason for the wearing of the sacred thread. The Pandit replied that the act of ritually wearing the sacred thread would enable him to embark upon a new life of high morals and noble deeds, as well as making him 'diwaj', twice-born. Upon receiving the Pandit's reply, Guru Nanak retorted that if the cheap cotton thread from a shop, which was prone to wear and tear, was lost, would it mean that the wearers of this so called sacred thread, Brahmins and Kashatriyas, had been divested of their faith and spiritual opportunity in this life? Was it the wearing of the sacred thread that sustained their faith or was the propriety of maintaining one's faith based on one's own principles, actions and deeds? The logic of Guru Nanak's questioning, perplexed the Pandit and disappointed his family, who had expended a good deal of money to arrange a feast to mark this important ceremonial occasion. Regardless, he refused to submit himself to this type of sacred thread wearing ceremony and challenged the Pandit to provide a sacred thread made of such constituents as:

'Make Mercy the cotton, Contentment the thread, Continence its knot, Truth its twists;
Such a sacred thread would be befitting for the Soul,
If you can produce this 'Janeu', O'Brahmin, then invest me with it'

Guru Nanak was the only male child and consequently his parents had nursed lofty aspirations regarding the future role of their son, in the family, community and business. Understandably, the symptoms of an unworldly, aloof and at times, outrageously unconventional attitude and behaviour were becoming a source of concern to his parents. In desperation, his father took the initiative in devising strategies in order to detract his son from his seemingly wayward course of steeped engrossment in and induct him in the ways of the world such as that of earning a living and caring for the family.

The second event, popularly known as 'Sacha Sauda—the True Enterprise', occurred when Guru Nanak's father gave him a sum of twenty rupees along with the instructions to visit a neighbouring city and pruchase some merchandise at a bargain, so that the retail price would yield a handsome profit. Thus fully briefed about spending the money wisely and profitably and accompanied by a family servant, Guru Nanak left for his business destination.

However, while on the way he came across a group of frail and haggard looking mendicants. Guru Nanak learnt that they had had no food for several days, whereupon, he spontaneously offered them all the money his father had given him for the business transaction. But the holy men refused to touch money for to do so would be contrary to their way of life, although they were willing to accept food. Hearing this, Guru Nanak rushed to the nearby town and freely expended all his money to buy food and with the aid of his servant personally delivered and served it to the hungry souls. Guru Nanak genuinely believed that the money thus spent was invested in a 'True and Profitable Enterprise', as it relieved hunger and human pain—an act of true benefaction and piety. Needless to say, upon learning the details of this his father was unable to appreciate the act of his son with the same degree of benevolence and charity of spirit.

During the succeeding years, Guru Nanak sought God in nature during his ramblings through forests and fields, he meditated on God's name in searching silence, he sang the glories and the indescribable greatness of God through hymns and he experienced irrespressible spiritual joy in talking about God, Humanity, Death, Ritual, purpose and goal of life and Man's actions and deeds, moral values and social relations, to young and old and to the holy and ungodly. As a last resort, his parents decided to ensnare him in worldliness by arranging to get him married. He fathered two sons but the marital and family attachments failed to deflect him from his chosen course of passionate love of God and humanity, and the search for Truth.

Eventually, he left his village and parental home to join government employment, as a store-keeper cum accountant, at a place called Sultanpur. He performed his official duties enthusiastically and conscientiously and soon won acclaim for his integrity and dilligence. He was a frugal man and only expended a small proportion of his salary that barely sufficed to meet his basic personal needs. Being a man of enormous compassion, he readily distributed the remanent portion of his salary among the poor and needy. His house soon became a noted centre of charity and daily congregational hymn-singing prayer meetings. Guru Nanak was very fond of music, so much so that he considered and allocated an important role to music in the proper exposition of his theology and mode of God's worship. Therefore, the hymns that he wrote, 974 in all, are a key to a particular frame of Indian classical music. He was ably assisted by a Muslim musican, bard and instrumentalist friend, called Mardana, from his old village. Mardana, the celestial 'Rabab-player' (a stringed instrument) joined him at Sultanpur and livened up the prayer sessions, served as personal attendant to Guru Nanak and thereafter remained his life-long associates. By now Guru Nanak's life was distinctly patterned on 'NAM', God's Name or Rememberance through prayer and meditation; 'DAN', spontaneous charity, almsgiving and the spirit of sharing; 'ISNAN', ablution, cleanliness and purity of human body; 'VAKHIAN', holding of spiritual and religious discourses and deputations amongst all religions; and 'GYAN', the search for divine knowledge and Truth, from wherever these could be learnt, gained or acquired.

It was at Sultanpur that while having his usual pre-dawn immersion in the rivulet 'Bein', Guru Nanak received his divine revelation directly from Almighty God at the age of 28 years. Thus armed with the blessings and Command of God Himself, Guru Nanak confidently heralded his global spiritual ministry, with the stirring and disturbingly unconventional declaration:

'There is no Hindu and no Musalman'

After declaring his holy ministry, Guru Nanak set off on extensive journeys, jouneying through not only the length and breadth of India but also touring

Tibet, Ceylon, Mecca, Medina in Arabia, Baghdad in Iraq, and Kabul in Afghanistan. During these wide-ranging travels, he met and held discussions with people of various religions and faiths, sects and nationalities. He learnt and taught as a world-teacher of new spiritual enlightenment, which he considered to be the common spiritual heritage of the entire humankind. His teachings were simple, direct and as, indeed, were his methods for conveying his message.

Pivotal Spiritual Concepts of Sikhism
Guru Nanak received the Divine Revelation and Mission directly from the Waheguru—the Wondrous Almighty God—Himself, during his mystical experience. Guru Nanak, through his vision and teachings, proved himself to be a seminal thinker, a religious philosopher, a boundlessly deep spiritual being, an ecumenical pioneer and an unrivalled crusader for remedying the ills of the humanity, who, as the founder of the Sikhism also chartered the framework of the fundamental Sikh/Khalsa beliefs and tenets.

Concept of God
The source for the well articulated idea and reality of God is Guru Granth Sahib, the Holy Scriptures, which begins with the key hymnal composition of Guru Nanak, called Japji Sahib—the Morning Prayer. Guru Nanak captioned the Japji Sahib with an utterly clear statement about the Sikh concept of God, in the Mool Mantra—the root and creedal affirmative statement of Sikhism about The One, Absolute, Transcendent, Supreme, Omnipotent, Omniscient, Immanent, Omnipresent, All Pervasive, Indwelling and Immortal God. It declares:—

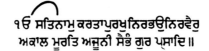

'Ik Onkar'
There is only ONE Supreme, Absolute, Transcendant Lord God.
'Sat Nam'
God's Name is Eternal Truth;
'Karta Purkh'
God is also Immanent and as such, he is the Sole Creator of all life and matter,
'Nirbhau Nirvair'
God is utterly Fearless and ever remains without hatred,
'Akal Murat'
God's being, existence and image is Timeless and Immortal, His All-Pervasive Spirit indwells all the known and unknown creation;
'Aujuni Saibhan'
God never takes human or any other form of Birth, nor does He ever perishes to the reborn. God is Self-Existent;
'Gur Parsad'
By the Guru's i.e. Lord God Himself, graciousness and spiritual awakening, God becomes known or is revealed to human beings.

Having unequivocally pinpointed the essentials about the idea and nature of God in the 'Mool Mantra', Guru Nanak continues:
'Jap'
Remember, Meditate and Worship the ONE LORD GOD:
'AD SACH'
Prior to the beginning of the Time itself, the Immortal, Ageless and Self-Existent God was, The Truth;
'Jugad Sach'
So throughout the Ages, since the Time itself found its existence, the Deathless God had ever been, The Truth;
'HAI BHI SACH'
Even now, The immanent God is, the Indestructable Truth;
'NANAK, HOSI BHI SACH'
Nanak says, for ever and ever The God shall eternally exist as the Prevalent and Immutable Truth and Imperishable Reality.

Oneness of God and Its manifestive Diversity and Implications
Therefore, the Sikh idea of God characterises Him with indivisible Unity and Oneness, Nirguna and Sauna, Creator, Sustainer, Destroyer, Supremely Sovereign, Eternal, Formless, Absolute, the Causes of Causes, Ineffable, both Immanent in His Creation and yet also remaining Transcendant, i.e., beyond

and apart from it, All Pervasive ... the list is inexhaustable. But despite this mind-boggling attributes, God is absolutely and uncompromisingly ONE, and being Peerless, He has no equals or partners. His Supreme ONENESS amidst the multiplicity of Creation is total, absolute, unchallenged and indivisible.

Guru Nank illustrates this point about the ONENESS and indivisible UNITY of GOD with many a simple metaphor, e.g.,

'Just as there are many seasons
But the sun that creates them is one,
So, O Nanak, the Creator assumes many garbs, but essentially is ONE'.

Again, he says
'God is like one vast lake in which blossom several varieties of water lilies'.

Continuing, Guru Nanak, adds,
'Thou hast only one face but so many masks Thou wearest,
To whom shall I pay homage? To whom make the offering of burning incense?'

Guru Nanak says,
'When all humankind has emanated from the ONE God, how can anybody dub human beings low or high'

Furthermore, Guru Nanak accorded full equality to women in every sphere of life, in medieval Indian society, which was aggressively and unjustly male dominated.

The Guru articulated his thoughts in the following hymn:—

'Of a woman are we conceived,
Of a woman we are born,
To a woman are we betrothed and married,
It is a woman who is a loyal friend and sharing partner in life,
It is a woman who keeps the human race going,
Through woman are established social ties.
Then how can or why should men consider
Womankind cursed and condemned,
When from woman are born leaders, rulers,
Saints, sages and prophets ....'

Sikhism emphasises the principle of 'respect for the individual and his or her human rights' and extends this attitude to all human beings and their systems of belief.

'Whilst living as active participants, in this world of human affairs and wordly activities, and leading a life full of laughter, play, and wearing good clothes, we can self-realise and redeem ourselves by following the path of devotional love for God and His humanity'.

In accordance with the basic Sikh/Khalsa belief about the Waheguru, idol-worship is strictly forbidden, along with graves, stones and effigies of other objects. The Sikh/Khalsa worship only the Maker and Creator of the Nature itself, the All-Pervading Waheguru. So the followers of Sikhism lost any fear of the forces of nature and developed a total disregard of superstition. This attitude led the Sikh/Khalsa to discard the ritualism and other related traditional practices. They refused to accept fatalistic philosophy of life and instead emerged as a self-made people.

There is no missionary movement in Sikhism, deliberately going out in the world of other faiths and atheism to seek converts. Guru Nanak asserted that people should practise their own faith, devoutly, since it matters little under what religious garb they seek their spiritual connection with the Source of all Creation, Waheguru. The Guru openly declares:

> 'The world is aflame, Lord, save it through Your Grace, and let
> Thy Humanity seek and obtain union with Thou by Whatever
> way or door it may approach Thee'

However, if anyone voluntarily wishes to tread the path laid down by Sikhism then that person is free to join the ranks of Khalsa/Sikhs by undergoing the appropriate initiation ceremony and expressly assenting to its code of discipline.

Finally, the attitude of Sikhism toward other religions and peoples is that of respect and mutual accomodation. Since it is utterly contrary to the Sikh faith, to hate and denigrate anyone or view, Sikhism offers ready tolerance even to its enemies.

Relationship between God and Humankind

The Sikh Scriptures stress this point: 'O My soul, thou hast issued forth from the Light of God; Know thy True essence and origin'; 'O my bodily vessel, when the Lord planteth His Own Light therein, then thou comest to life'. Therefore, human life in its origin is as pure and as good as the Creator, the source of all life, Himself.

Regarding the privilege of human birth, Guru says: 'Thou hast come into a human form, this is thy only opportunity to meet your God'

So it is in human existence that we can best strive to reach our destined goal, which is, to achieve Union with God, since Waheguru has invested us with pure soul, which is part of the Master Soul Itself, free-will, intellect and alternative paths to God, or Truth.

The obdurate hurdle that sets our soul apart from Waheguru is the sinful tendency and volatility of 'Haumain', Ego, generating in us the sense of the 'I-Amness', 'Self-centredness' and utter 'Selfishness'. This Ego is undoubtedly the root of all known sins: since it profusely breeds the five arch-enemies of the human soul, 'Kam', Lust and carnal cravings: 'Karodh', Wrath or Anger;

'Lobh', Avarice or Selfish-Greed; 'Moh', Undue Attachment to worldly network of personal relationships and material artifacts; and, 'Hankar', Pride, haughtiness, and conceit. But Guru adds that although:

'Ego is the fatal disease of the soul,
Yet its remedial antidote also resides therein'

Under the blessed guidance of the Guru, the obverse and positive side of the Ego can be channalised side to still the restive mind and gradually prepare it through discipline approach to receive for the mystic experience which reveals the Waheguru. The control of the fanciful flights of the human mind are essential prerequisites for spiritual progress, and the difficulties in the realisation of this objective are highlighted in Guru Nanak's Japji Sahib:

'Conquest of one's mind results in conquering the World'

But how can the soul and mind demolish the barrier of delusion in order to unite or merge with Waheguru, which, according to Sikhism is the ultimate spiritual goal of human life? Guru Nanak raises and answers this question in Japji Sahib:

'How then shall the Truth be known?
How the veil of false illusion torn?
O Nanak, thus runneth the writ divine,
Abide by His Will and make it thine.'

But, again, how can we understand and act accordingly to Waheguru's Will? Apart from Guru's guidance, we need to invoke the 'Nam', the Loving Name of Waheguru to such an extent that its spiritual vibrations constantly permeate and totally possess our conscious and unconcious being. Added to this is the acceptance of God's Will, which demands total and uncomplaining submission on our part.

Another related objective of human life is to permanently break the unceasing cycle of birth, death and rebirth, the cosmic process of the transmigration of the soul. Waheguru grants us an opportunity by bestowing human life upon us to break this vicious sequence and attain perfect union with Him. Once we are absorbed in Him, we attain liberation from this otherwise unending transmigratory cycle.

Sikhism adapted the theory of Karma, according to which we receive the rewards or punishment for acts committed in our previous lives. But to terminate this ceaseless cyclic process, Guru Advises, the 'Gurmukhs', God-Conscious, to spontaneously engage in the pursuit of Truth, contentment, kindness and faith. Even the crushing burden of sins accumulated in our past lives can be washed away by the 'Nadar', Grace of Waheguru, 'in a twinkling of an eye'.

The Guru in Sikhism

The spiritual role and guidance of the Guru is of paramount importance in Sikh/Khalsa thought. The Guru is not an intercessor between the Sikh/Khalsa and the Waheguru, because in Sikhism one does not need an intermediary, between a human being and his Maker. Rather the role of the Guru is to keep the Sikh/Khalsa on the straight and narrow path of Truth, assist him to discover the Truth for himself, instil fear of Waheguru in him which gradually sprouts as love of God, and serve as a spiritual mentor.

The Guru through spiritual self-realization possesses the deepest knowledge of Waheguru, which he willingly and lovingly shares with his Sikh/Khalsa. The Guru, in Sikhism, is NOT God. Guru Nanak says: 'Take him as Guru who shows you the path of Truth: who tells you of the One, of whom nothing is known: who tells you of the Divine Word.' Therefore, the Guru can be the mouthpiece of God but still he is a mortal being and not a divine God; he is to be loved, respected and consulted but definitely not worshipped; he is essentially a divinely-inspired philosopher, spiritual guide and teacher. Above all, the Guru is not a re-incarnation of God or in any way related to Him except spiritually. Guru Nanak has referred to himself in his hymns as the bard, slave, servant and even the dog of God. The Guru actively guided the Sikh/Khalsa to become 'Gurmukh', the God-Awakened Being, by treading the 'Gurmat Marg', the path laid down for the Sikh/Khalsa.

Five Sikh/Khalsa Ideals

Five fundamental Ideals encompass the structural and institutional aspects of the Sikhism and the Sikh/Khalsa Way of Life.

First, 'Nam Japna'—sincere and devotional worship of the Name of the Waheguru, the Lord God. According to Guru Nanak, the true hallmark of the spiritual and religious life of a person can be judged from the intensity, love and passion with which one remembers Waheguru's Name and experiences His Presence in his own heart, mind and soul. The rememberance of Waheguru's Name is not to be practised in the form of rote-learning or mechanical repetition in a meaningless way. The real essence of this ideal is to understand the meaning and the spiritual import of the words of the prayer and deliberately adopt these as the permanent rules of life.

Guru Nanak tirelessly exhorts the Sikh/Khalsa, 'Nam' is worth more than all pilgrimages to so-called holy rivers and places, because while worshipping 'Nam', we delve into our own heart and being which are the shrines of God and the sanctury of divine knowledge'. He eloquently expresses his own experience of following the path of Nam: 'As the blind use a stick, so do I use and rely on the Divine Nam of the Lord to feel the path that leads me to God'. Again, Guru Nanak stresses, 'I have no miracles except the Nam of Waheguru'. Without the Nam of Waheguru, we are nothing more than 'merely moving corpses'. Therefore, for the Sikh/Khalsa there is no greater gift that can be secured in this life than the blessings of the 'Nam' of Waheguru; since 'Nam' is the Supreme remedy for all the ills of the human soul. But the vast majority of us desperately need the spiritual guidance of the Guru and the Grace of the Incomparable Waheguru to instill and cultivate 'Nam' in our psyche.

Sikh/Khalsa Mode and Form of Worship
Because of the overwhelming importance of the gift of the divine 'Nam' of Waheguru, Guru has laid out a well disciplined path and routine for the Sikh/Khalsa to faithfully follow.

Since the Sikh/Khalsa concept of God confirms that Waheguru is Omnipresent and Immanent, therefore, we can pray to the Almightly Lord anywhere and at any time. But pray we unfailingly must. Guru Says, 'Pray to Waheguru, through His 'Nam', while up and about, asleep, awake or in whatever state'. However, in the experience of the Guru the best time for prayer is 'Amrit Vela', during the stillness of the pre-dawn ambrosial hours. Guru Nanak advised the Sikh/Khalsa to rise at 'Armrit Vela' i.e. before dawn and endeavour to establish communion with Waheguru.

A Sikh/Khalsa is admonished to practise the 'Nam Simran', remembering and mediating upon the 'Nam' of Waheguru, with every breath that he inhales or exhales from his body. Futhermore, he must understandingly read daily and eventually know by heart the set five prayer compostions. The prayer hymns that should be recited in the morning are Japji Sahib of Guru Nanak, Jap Sahib of Guru Gobind Singh, Swaiyas, and those for the evening are Rehras Sahib, including Chaupai and Swaiyas and Anand Sahib (Prayer of Bliss). Lastly Kirtan Sohala is recited just before retiring for the night. These prayers are recited at the individual level or amongst the family.

GURDWARA—the Sikh/Khalsa Place of Worship
The most important aspect of the Sikh/Khalsa prayer and worship is when it is held in congretational form at the 'Gurdwara', the Sikh Place of Worship.

Gurdwara is the hub institution of Sikhism. The collective strength of the Sikh people is centred in and revolves around the Gurdwara. There is no other comparable place of worship which can possibly match the potency or importance of the Gurdwara, since it unleashes, injects and renews fresh strength and purpose in the collective and individual lives of the Sikh/Khalsa. Wherever the Sikhs go, even in small numbers, their top priority is the establishment of the Gurdwara. There is no sacrifice that is too great for the Sikh/Khalsa to make for their Gurdwara. Congregational meetings are held in

Gurdwaras, mainly on Sundays in the West because it is the traditional day of rest, not that it is a holy day since Sikhs regard any day as being equally holy and good, as long as we remember the 'Waheguru' and practise righteousness.

The main elements of the congregational worship in the Gurdwara, Guru's Door, are the performance of 'Kirtan', musical rendition and presentation of Guru's Hymns by adept Kirtan 'Ragis', Guru's hymn singers; lectures and talks on religious and historical themes and topics; readings of 'Gurbani', Guru's hymns, from the Guru Granth Sahib, the Holy Sikh Scriptures. The Sikh/Khalsa congregation is called 'Sadh Sahib', the congregation of saints, and it consists of both women and men. Traditionally the menfolk sit on one side of the prayer hall and the womenfolk occupy seats on the other side. This apparent sex segregation is a cultural anachronism and does not have any Sikh/Khalsa religious sanction. The atmosphere in the Worship hall is agreeably pleasant and informal. The worship and prayers carry on for three or four hours but everybody is free to come or leave the Gurdwara at their own convenience.

Inside the prayer hall, the 'Sadh Sangat', the Sikh congregation, is seated on a well carpeted floor. There are two reasons for the congregation having to sit on the ground. Firstly, as a mark of respect, the Sadh Sangat must sit at a lower level than that occupied by the Guru, that is , Guru Granth Sahib, the Holy Sikh Scriptures. Secondly, the act of sitting at the same level is a symbolic and meaningful gesture to emphasize and the Sikh/Khalsa ideal of equality—Sisterhood and Brotherhood of humankind. In the Guru's House, Gurdwara, everybody is equal and, therefore, is equally worthy of the same consideration as anybody else, irrespective of any distinction of caste, class, creed, colour, nationality, social, economic and occupational status. The non-sikh visitors are always welcome in the Gurdwara and are invariably accorded civility, courtesy and hospitality.

However, it is obligatory for Sikhs and non-Sikhs alike to strictly observe certain rules of action and propriety of whilst in the Gurdwara.

Apart from being a place of Sikh worship, the Gurdwara houses facilities for teaching the Panjabi language and rudiments of the Sikh religion to the young children; Sikh weddings are solemnised therein and various other community affairs and activities also take place. It provides a centralised community centre for informal social, individual and collective, meetings and gatherings of the Sikh/Khalsa, hence, it performs a vital social function at the ommunity and individual levels particulary in the foreign countries.

'Guru Ka Langar'—Guru's Free Community Kitchen

'Guru Ka Langar', is known in short as 'Langer', is a significant Sikh/Khalsa institution and ever since the inception of the Sikhism, it has remained an inseparable part of the Gurdwara. The word 'Free' means that no charge is made for the meals and other items of hospitality provided, and that no one, be he or she a Sikh or non-Sikh, is barred from eating the food provided. It is important that the diners in the 'Langar' must only take that amount of food issued in the 'Guru Ka Langar', must not be waste because such wastage is an expression of self indulgence and shows lack of consideration and concern for the sanctified food, a scarce resource, and needs of humanity.

The Sikh Gurus enthusiastically built and developed the institution of Langar because of their firm belief that if the devotees of the Sikh/Khalsa faith, hailing from all social strata as well as creeds of society, could learn to sit together and break bread, the great gift of Waheguru, then they would be welded into a casteless and classless fraternity. This practical and down to earth vision and approach of the Sikh Gurus brought into being the fundamental Sikh/Khalsa twin concept of 'Sangat and Pangat', that is while participating in Sikh worship and prayer the congregation formed 'Sadh Sangat'—the unified gathering of the spiritually initiated God-Adoring and Humanity-Loving Saint Soldiers—and its complimentary half, the 'Pangat' i.e., literally, sitting in a row, partaking food in Langar, Guru's Free Community Kitchen, as brothers, sisters and full-fledged partners in the perfect and spirit of Equality, Humility and reciprocal love.

'Langar' and type of Meals served therein

It is important to note that the Sikh/Khalsa are not wholly vegetarians. They can and do eat meat, (unless one turns to vegetarianism because of personal preference or force of habit) providing the meat is 'Jhatka meat', meaning that the animal has been slaughtered by a swift stroke of the sword or other weapon so that animal does not undergo lingering pain and suffering. Amongst certain section of the Sikhs there is an ongoing controversy regarding the type of animal whose flesh can be eaten, or even whether one should eat meat at all. But from the Sikh/Khalsa religious viewpoint, it can be reasonably ascertained by references to Scriptural authority that there is no such taboo. Guru Nanak amply illustrates these points in his hymns, and commenting on the idea of impurity or unholiness about food and eating, says: "Water, the very first element which is life-breeding and life-preserving, contains live organisms, which the humans use to clean themselves and sustain themselves; how can one totally observe the germ or life-free purtiy when one's food, like every grain of corn, crops and vegetation, is replete with the observable and unseen life." Guru Nanak calls the excessively morbid preoccupation with the idea of purity and impurity in food matters as, 'superstition and being led astray in a different unavailing cul-de-sac'. Continuing he adds, 'to consume every edible gift of God, that He has provided for our sustenance, is a pure act'. However, he warns against gluttony and exhorts us 'To avoid eating and drinking those items of food which arouse base passions in us, benumb our human faculties and are injurious to our health'. The question often arises, should the Sikh/Khalsa eat beef? There is no explicit or implicit Sikh religious injunction forbidding the Sikhs/Khalsa to eat beef. Nevertheless, many Sikh/Khalsa are still under the centuries old cultural spell of Hinduism, regard the flesh of the 'sacred' cow as something of a taboo.

As such, in deference to the wider spectrum of sensiblities of one and all and to preserve the environmental sanctity of Gurdwara, only vegetarian meals are prepared and served there to Sikh congregations.

Guru Granth Sahib—the Sacred Scriptures
The singular source of the Sikh/Khalsa spirituality and theology is indisputably centred in the divinely-inspired hymnal verses that were composed by the Sikh Gurus. It all started with Guru Nanak, a superb poet, linguist and seer of rare distincition, who composed, uttered, sang and recorded his soul-stirring spiritual and metaphysical poetry. Guru Nanak says: "As the Almighty Master, Lord God, bestows His gift of Divine Word upon me, so I ecstatically utter His Word at His Command". Thus, his poetical writings were destined to form the solid spiritual nucleus of the Guru Granth Sahib—the Holy Sikh Scriptures. The succeeding Sikh Gurus faithfully followed his precept and example and, in their turn, considerably augmented the stock of spiritual poetry. However, the honour, responsibility and task of compiling, composing and editing the Guru Granth Sahib fell upon the Fifth Sikh Guru, Arjan, who was a prolific author of poetical compositions, a profound thinker-saint. He ceremoniously installed the 'Adi Granth' first or original edition of the Holy Scriptures of the Sikhs, at the Golden Temple, Amritsar, in 1604 A.D. Finally, Guru Gobind Singh, the tenth and last Sikh Guru, in 1708 A.D., ended the system and line of and Gurus in Sikhism and decreed that, thenceforth, "All the Sikh/Khalsa are to regard the Sacred Sikh Scriptures as their ONLY GURU, and acknowledge It as the tangible spiritual personification of all the Gurus. Whomsoever sincerely seeks to establish communion with Waheguru—the All-Pervasive God—may approach and discover HIM through the Divine Word incorporated in the Guru Granth Sahib". Ever since, the Guru Granth Sahib has remained the Eternal Guru, Spiritual Guide, of the Sikh/Khalsa and consequently the Sikh people have always considered and accepted it as the embodiment of the 'Living Spirit' of the Gurus themselves.

Understandably, Guru Granth Sahib is the exclusive source of the Sikh/Khalsa prayer and worship and as such Its physical entity has become an object of extreme reverence. The fundamental Sikh/Khalsa belief affirms that Guru Granth Sahib emblematizes the ever-living spirit of the Sikh Gurus, whose hymnal compostions, are collectively called 'Gurbani'—the divinely-inspired spiritual utterances of the Sikh Gurus.

95

The Sacred Sikh Scriptures contain hymns written by the saints and seers of other religions, e.g., Hindus and Muslims, who came from various parts of the Indian sub-Continent. The Guru Granth Sahib consists of nearly six thousand hymns of varying length and poetical metre, and their arrangement has been categorised under specific Indian classical or light classical musical measures and melody. The vast number of hymns have been composed in the medieval Panjabi language, written in the Gurmukhi script. Nevertheless, in keeping with their spirit and vision, the Sikh Gurus made liberal use of other Indian and Asian languages, like Sanskrit, Persian and Arabic. The devout Sikh/Khalsa, before starting their working day approach Guru Granth Sahib and open It at random. The Hymn starting on the top of the left hand page is read, it is known as 'HUKAM LENA'-seeking the guidance of the spiritual Command from the Guru. It has a specific message and import for the true seeker of Truth and the faithful.

Upon 'Gurparabas'—special Sikh/Khalsa occasions of celebration concerned with the lives of the Sikh Gurus—'AKHAND PATH' is performed, meaning the non-stop and uninterrupted reading of the entire volume of the Guru Granth Sahib by a relay of readers; and it takes approximately forty eigth hours to complete the reading of Its 1430 pages.

'Prem or Bhau'—All-encompassing Universal LOVE
Guru Nanak says: 'While I remember Waheguru—'NAM JAPNA'—I live and the moment He is forgotten, I suffer instant death'. The practical and sincere manifestation of this Ideal Love includes the unselfish love of God and also entails loving His Creation. For the sake of this ideal the devotee must be prepared to make any sacrifice unhesitatingly and unreservedly, and remain in absolute submission to the Will of God. Guru Nanak says: "Whomsoever has learnt the art of sincere and intensive Love, obtains union with Waheguru".

'SEWA'—performance of Self-less Service and Active beneficence
The third ideal of Sikhism is Sewa. In order to serve Waheguru, the human being must disinterestedly serve humankind in whatever way he or she can. The Guru says: 'While performing 'SEWA'—selfless service—in the right spirit, the human being is freed from the scare of failings and weaknesses, and such a person obtains the grace of the Waheguru'. All the Sikh Gurus set a personal example in the Langar by serving the Sikh/Khasla with meals, removing and cleaning the used dishes, sweeping the floor, fetching water and fuel for the Langar and by fanning the Sangat, the Sikh congregation in hot weather.

'KIRAT KARNI'—Engage in creative, productive and honest labour
The fourth ideal of the Sikh/Khalsa Way of Life is 'Kirat Karni', meaning the earning of one's livelihood by honest means and diligently working for one's wages, salary or remuneration. Sikhism condemns indolence or idleness and tendency to live off others as parasitic. The Sikh Gurus fully realised the importance of being gainfully employed in an honest vocation, as it built up the self confidence and dignity of the workers; brought economic independence and stability into family and social life; provided means for establishing the Sikh/Khalsa institutions and, above all, because it lessened the chances of a class of social dregs appearing on the scene. According to the Gurus comments, there is no job or occupation that is to be shunned by the Sikh/Khalsa, as long as it conforms to ethical principles, legal, and does not fleece others. The exaction of excessive profit and the relentless pursuance of the theory of 'Englightened Self-Interest' at the expense of others, is emphatically outlawed. Again the emphasis is on 'balance' and harmony and a conscious avoidance of extremes in all human affairs. As such, a sane, sensible and practicable Way of Life is laid down.
Guru comments, 'For the God-Concious and Righteous person every type of work or profession is acceptable providing such work is in conformity with the moral principles.' Guru Nanak says, 'Excessive accumulation of wealth is only possible when one resorts to unjust and immoral means to obtain it; but such pools of treasures shall not accompany one after death.' He further adds, 'Anybody who usurps the right or wealth of others must be regarded, as the flesh of the cow to a Hindu and flesh of a swine is to a Muslim, a sinful act'.

'WAND SHAKNA'—Open and untrammelled Spirit of Charity
The fifth ideal of Sikhism, 'Wand Shakna', radiates the inherent humanitarian spirit compellingly bidding the Sikh/Khalsa to display concrete and practical concern for the needs and requirements of the less well-off, under-priviledged, indigent and deprived sections of human race. Guru Nanak states, 'Having earned wages as a due reward of honest labour, we must dutifully share the surplus with others'. The compensation for this charitable spirit of the Sikh/Khalsa will accrue thus: 'Those who earn a living by the sweat of their brow, and willingly share it with others, Nanak says, shall discover and get to know the righteous path to true living'. The Sikh Gurus have laid down that every Sikh/Khalsa must donate at least one tenth of his/her income or other sources of wealth for the benefit of society.

Guru Nanak's Methods
Guru Nanak adopted Socratic lines of approach since he avoided, as far as possible, offending the feelings of the people he conversed with. His comments

at his initiation demonstrates this fact. During his travels in India and abroad, he formed a network of meaningful relationships with many religions and peoples, and established centres where persons of his own spiritual and religious persuasion could meet and prosper.

Guru Nanak founded the Kartar Pur, meaning the Abode of the Creator, which became the centre for the realisation of the proto-type Sikh ideal of human being and Sikh society. The dwellers of this colony worked during the day and congregated twice daily, in the early morning and evening for prayer and worship. The ideal person in Sikhism became 'Gur mukh' or 'GurSikh'— God-oriented and humanity loving the Saint-Soldier. The aggregate of Saint-Soldiers of 'Gurmukhs' formed a new type of Sikh/Khalsa society.

Guru Nanak did not believe in renunciation, asceticism or self-mortification or penance as a means of enlightenment. His philosophy of spiritual life was: 'Be in the world but not worldly'. For securing freedeom from worldly allurements, he commanded:

> *'The lotus in the water is not wet*
> *Nor the water-fowl in the stream.*
> *If a human being would live, but by the world uncontaminated,*
> *Meditate and ever repeat the Name of the Lord Supreme.'*
> *And this can best be done, in 'Sadh Sangat'.*

In other words, for leading a righteous life one has consciously to find the correct balance between the wordly and spiritual planes of life.

Five stages of Spiritual Progression in the Sikh faith
In Japji Sahib Guru Nanak specifies Five Stages of Spiritual growth. The steps by which a human being can progress to spiritual elevation and enlightenment start from the planet earth, which is called 'Dharma Khanda'—the Realm of Law. Then one proceeds to acquire learning and knowledge in 'Gyan Khanda'—the Realm of Knowledge. Thereafter, one enters into the 'Sarm Khanda'—the Realm of Beauty. Thenceforward, one is elevated to the 'Karama Khanda'—the Realm of Action. Finally, comes 'Sach Khanda'—the Realm of Truth—and is blessed with the inseparable union with Waheguru, the Lord Supreme God. In order to achieve this ultimate level of spiritual perfection and divine englightenment, the individual will have to practise the following priciples: Self control; Patience; Knowledge; Love and Fear of Waheguru, God; and constant Earnest Prayer.

Role and Place of Human Reason in Sikhism
Guru Nanak does not recommend blind faith in one's search for the realisation of Waheguru, and as such he emphasises the place of human intelligence and reason as follows: 'Use your itelligence in serving God and in gaining merit;

use your brain to read and understand what you read and how you give in charity. This is the only way; the rest is the doing of devil'. Those who do not use their brains and intelligence to unravel the secrets of the Divine Word are castigated by Guru Nanak as 'real donkeys'.

Thus Guru Nanak laid the foundations of a New Model of Man and Society. Every Sikh is to be a 'Gurmukh' of 'Gur Sikh', i.e., a Saint-Soldier and an enlightened being, and Sikh society characterised by such qualities as Saintliness in character, martial in spirit, and scholarly and englightened in 'Gurmat'—Divine Knowledge.

Spiritual Successor Appointed by Guru Nanak
Shortly before his death, in 1539 A.D., Guru Nanak took the momentous decision to appoint a successor. The criteria that he applied in the final selection of his successor was on the basis of absolute obedience and perfection in spiritual attainment and enlightenment. Thus Guru Nanak established the principle of 'Spiritual Meritocracy' to be rigidly and uncompromisingly applied for the appointment of his successor Sikh Guru and this was faithfully followed by the succeeding nine Gurus of the Sikh/Khalsa.

Institutionalised Democracy in Sikhism
Guru Nanak had two sons and both of them staked claims to the Guruship, not upon the basis of merit alone but basically on heredity. Instead Guru Nanak chose one of his Sikhs, renaming him as 'Angad'—meaning of one's own limb or part—and bestowed the spiritual office of the Sikh/Khalsa Guruship upon him for his qualities of direct character and leadership. As a direct consequence of this democratic act, there emerged new, organisational aspects of Sikhism. It forged a Sprital Unity and established Democratic Equality between the mentor, i.e., the Guru, and his Sikh, i.e., the disciple. Both, the leader and the follower, were at par with each other, and this ensured the pristine continuity and future growth and development of Sikhism. All the Ten Sikh Gurus, after assuming spirtual leadership, never used their personal names in their writings and hymnal compositions. Instead, they referred to themselves as the, Second, Third, Fouth, Fifth ..... 'NANAK', and throughout their lives exhibited an uncanny 'Unity of Thought and Life of Action'. Therefore, in Sikhism, the Ten Sikh Gurus are regarded as the embodiments of the same 'Spiritual Essence and Vision', the attributes that are amply demonstrated and confirmed by their ideal deeds and exemplary lives. However, the Sikh Gurus were not incarnations of one another in any sense or manner.

Since, the democratic spirit and processes have become an inseparable part of the Sikh/Khalsa body politic and organisation life, Gurdwaras are managed by the democratically elected representative Executive committees and every member of the Sikh/Khalsa community, woman or man, has an inalienable right to have a say in the running of all organisations, religious or secular.

Guru Nanak's Successors
The Master Architect of the Sikhism, Guru Nanak, was followed by nine equally worthy and extraordinarily gifted successors, who in their turn remained tenaciously loyal to the basic framework of Sikhism as laid down by the First Guru, but also made their own unique contribution to the Sikh/Khalsa Way of Life. Their names in chronological order as follows:

Guru Angad

Guru Amardas

Guru Ramdas — he founded the City of Amritsar

Guru Arjan — he edited the Sikh Holy Book, the *Guru Granth Sahib,* and built at Amritsar the Golden Temple known as *Darbar Sahib*

Guru Hargobind — he founded the Sikh/Khalsa militia

Guru Har Rai

Guru Har Krishan

Guru Teg Bahadour

Guru Gobind Singh

The last and the Tenth Guru of Sikh/Khalsa was, Guru Gobind Singh, a towering multi-faceted personality and genius. He possessed the hall-mark of 'Royal Courage', which remained unyielding in the face of all adversity. The development and formative phases through which Sikhism had passed under the guidance and leadership of the preceding Gurus reached their fulfilment during the Guruship of Guru Gobind Singh. Two crowning and historic achievements of Guru Gobind are specifially noteworthy. Firstly, he established the 'Immortal Order of the Khalsa' in 1699 A.D; Secondly, he ended the line and practice of succession by Gurus, and instead, installed the Guru Granth Sahib—the Sacred Sikh Scriptures—as spiritual and guide the authority of the Sikh/Khalsa. The responsibility for leadership in secular affairs was vested in a democratically elected group consisting of Five Saint-Soldiers.

There has never since been any need or opportunity for another 'human' Guru, as clearly understood in the Sikh/Khalsa context, since 1708 A.D. to lead the community. Because, Guru Granth Sahib is the ultimate and perpetual spiritual guide of the Sikh/Khalsa, their secular, community and national affairs have to be managed by democratically elected representatives from amongst the Khalsa Panth— Sikh/Khalsa community and nation.

Guru Gobind Singh and the 'KHALSA'

The KHALSA—the Holy Fraternity or Order of Universal Brotherhood, a truly unique creation in the religious, spiritual and social history of the world, was formally instituted at Anandpur, City of Bliss, by Guru Gobind Singh on 30th March, 1699 A.D., which according to the Indian calendar marks the First day of the month Vaisakh, ushering in the Sikh New Year. Guru Gobind Singh had summonded the followers of Sikhism from all over the country to congregate at Anandpur on the 'Vaisakhi Day', and just before inaugurating the Holy Brotherhood of the Khalsa, through the 'Amrit Shakna', the Khalsa initiation ceremony, he decided to put the Sikhs to a stern final test. After the morning prayers and worship were over, Guru Gobind Singh stood up in front of the huge gathering and unsheathing his sword issued a dramatic demand in these words: 'Is there anybody in this congregation who is willing to offer his head for the sake of the Guru and religion?' The crowd froze, paralysed with fear. However, one man did manage to gather his wits and offered his head unconditionally to the Guru. Guru Gobind Singh took him into a tent and from inside came the audible thud of a sword stroke and a gush of blood. Such a goary spectacle was more than sufficient for a large number of the congregation to disperse hastily. At that instant, Guru Gobind Singh reappeared and much to the consternation of the still present members of his audience repeated his call for yet another head. When five devotees came through this trial Guru Gobind Singh amazed the crowd by fetching the Five Fearless devotees, who had willingly staked of their lives for the sake of the religion and righteousness, dressed in colourful uniforms, beturbanned and bearded, with their swords of honour. Thus chosen, the 'Immortal Five' were called 'Panj Piaras'—Five Beloved Ones—by the Guru and they were dressed and equipped exactly as the Guru himself. They were imbued with the traits of the Guru's own personality. Then Guru Gobind Singh prepared 'Khande Ka Amrit'—Life-giving Nectar, obtained by stirring water and sugar crystals in a steel bowl with a double-edged sword and accompanied by a recitation of five hymns —and ceremoniously administered it to the 'Panj Piaras' in order to initiate them into the Holy Order of the Brotherhood of Khalsa. The Five initiates had to drink 'Khande Ka Amrit' from the same bowl, and this symbolic act instilled, fostered and emphasized the brotherly spirit of belonging and equality amongst them. Afterwards, Guru Gobind Singh also took the 'Pahul' or 'Khanda Ka Amrit' from the 'Panj Piaras', thus eradicating any difference between them and himself. Thus, was created the true model of the ideal 'Saint-Soldier',based on the democratic and moral foundations of Sikh/Khalsa society.

Khalsa/Sikh Code of Discipline and the Mandatory 'Articles of Faith'

Upon joining the Holy Order of the Khalsa Brotherhood, every member takes a vow to faithfully observe the prescribed Khalsa/Sikh Code of Discipline and the consequent Articles of Faith. There is NO dispensation from this code for anybody and as such there are no half-way houses for the members of the Khalsa. In other words, one is either a full member of the Khalsa by precept and practice or one is not. The Khalsa is obliged to be equipped with the following five prescribed religious symbols; each starts with the letter 'K':

'Kes'—the uncut, untrammelled and natural length 'HAIR' on the head, and for the males a full beard and moustache.

Every Khalsa/Sikh is absolutely forbidden, regardless of the circumstances, to cut, shave, trim, singe, pluck or in any other way defile the natural hair from any part of her or his body. Male Sikhs must wear a 'TURBAN'—the only permissable, obligatory form of head-dress.

'Kanga'—a small wooden comb to be carried in head hair.

'Kara'—a steel round-shaped, bangle-like object to be worn on the right wrist.

'Karpan'—a small symbolic sword mounted in a special purpose-made, sling-like scabbard called, 'Gatra'.

'Kasha'—a garment approximating to a Boxer's or just ordinary shorts but made to a specific design to be used either as underpants or, depending on the weather or occasion, just by itself.

There are Four religious injunctions which must never be violated:

First is the sanctified significance of the 'HAIR':a Khalsa must not cut or remove hair from the head, face or any other part of the physical frame.

The second injunction stresses the moral and ethical purity of the Khalsa/Sikh Way of Life: a Khalsa must not commit adultery. The sanctity of human relationship between two people within the framework of a properly constituted marriage must always be upheld. Guru Gobind Singh says: 'One must not, even in a dream, join another in sexual overtures, to whom he or she is not married'.

The third binding imperative forbids the Khalsa to smoke or chew any type of tobacco or kindred substances. Furthermore, the Khalsa must not drink or consume alcohol, opium, wine or any other intoxicant. These corrupt the human mind. Tobacco was shunned by the Khalsa because it was considered injurious to health, created nauseating odours, polluted the air and generated lethargy.

The fouth Khalsa/Sikh injuction affirms humane concern and respect for all life, especially for the dumb creatures who cannot fend for themselves. The Khalsa is prohibited to eat meat of a 'Ritually killed' animal. As mentioned elsewhere, the Khalsa/Sikh can eat meat as long as the animal is killed by one swift stroke of the sword, called 'Jhatka', or by any other device minimising the animal's suffering.

Significance of the Five Khalsa/Sikh 'Articles of Faith'

First, 'Kes', the undesecrated full length hair represents a readily recognisable physical characteristic of a saintly human personality. It provides the tangible emblem of the Khalsa personality. 'Kes' are the Guru's seal of affirmation on the physical being of the Khalsa. In the view of the high regard for the 'Kes', the Khalsa is clearly instructed to keep the hair clean by washing it every week or as often as necessary. External cleanliness is as important for the Khalsa as internal purity.

It is very essential to understand the actual nature and importance of the Khalsa/Sikh 'TURBAN', particularly for people in the West. The Khalsa/Sikh 'Turban' is the integral concomitant of the 'Kes'; therefore, it cannot and must not be compared or equated with any other type or form of head gear. The Khalsa/Sikhs wear the Turbans not as a matter of fashion, habit, custom or social trend, but because they are categorically enjoined upon to wear the Turban as a religious duty.

To sum up the uniqueness of these religious symbols:

The Khalsa/Sikh 'TURBAN', also respectfully called 'Dastar', is alive insignia representing the continuity and perpetuation of a unified relationship with the immanent spirit and personality of the Great Master, Guru Gobind Singh himself.

Second, the 'Kanga', a small head-comb made of wood, symbolises 'Purity' and cleanliness. The Khalsa/Sikh must comb their hair, and beards, where applicable, at least twice daily.

Third, 'Kara', the all-steel bangle worn on the right wrist, stands for the total submission to the Supreme Will of the Waheguru, Lord God. It should also serve as a stern reminder that they must not commit misdeeds. Being a circular object, without beginning or end, it symbolises Waheguru, God, in the centre, with humankind placed equidistant upon at the circumference. Therefore, it asserts the concept of the indivisible Unity and Oneness of the Waheguru and the spiritual equality and relationship amongst the human races.

Fourth, 'Karpan', a reasonably small sword, is the standard equipment of the Saint-Soldier, i.e., the Khalsa/Sikh. It represents honour and provides means for the protection of personal or oppressed humanity's honour. It must never be drawn in anger or vindictiveness. It is an emblem of the Soldier of Waheguru. It has its ceremonial uses in the Gurdwara. The Khalsa/Sikh 'Karpan' is an essential religious token sanctioned by Guru Gobind Singh and the right of the Khalsa/Sikh to have it on their person has been acknowledged in India and many other countries, since it is an integral part of their religious discipline.

Fifth, 'Kasha', a pair of shorts cum underwear, is symbolic moral restraint of the Khalsa/Sikhs. It teaches the rudiments of self-control and suppression of excessive sexual desires. Of course, it has its mundane usages as well, e.g., in hot climates, it is a comfortable garment to wear. Besides, as compared with some of the cumbersome clothes worn in India, the 'Kasha' facilitates agility and freedom of physical movement.

Finally, the faithful and truly loyal Khalsa/Sikh does not need or require elaborate reasons for wearing and maintaining his or her 'Articles of Faith', as listed above. It is more than sufficient for the committed Saint-Soldier to give obedience to the Guru's Command and unquestionably emulate the traits he personified and bade his followers to adopt.

Khalsa/Sikh Names

The Khalsa/Sikh names, both for males and females, are determined by their Sikh religion itself. Every name has two constituents, first the personal name and second, the last name. There is a fair degree of latitude in the selection issued by Guru Gobind Singh. Sikhism had been crusading against the rigidities, injustices and inequalities of the caste System, characterised by from four major elements in the Caste System, namely, lineage, occupation, social status in the hierarchy and the religious heritage. The 'Amrit Dhari'—the duly initiated—Khalsa/Sikhs had to take a vow to relinquish their past caste associations. The names based on caste and sub-caste readily identified a person's social group or status. Guru Gobind Singh gave the last name of 'Singh' meaning 'Lion', to all Sikh/Khalsa males and 'Kaur', meaning 'Princess', to all the females; being forbidden by him to use one's caste or sub-caste names. The effective practice is to use the first and last name together, e.g., Kirpal Singh. Once understood, there is no need for anybody to get confused about the Khalsa/Sikh names. The correct way to address Khalsa/Sikh male, is 'Sardar' and female, 'Sardarni'.

Khalsa/Sikh Social ceremonies and customs

Soon after the birth of a child the parents take him or her to the Gurdwara, offer prayers for the longevity of the child's life and seek the scriptural of the blessings Guru Granth Sahib, the Sikh holy book. They also seek the first or personal name of the child from the pages of the Guru Granth Sahib. It is done by opening the Scriptures at random and the first letter of the hymn on the left hand page is taken as the first alphabet of the child's personal name.

The marriage ceremony is performed in the Gurdwara. The bride and the bridegroom are seated in front of the Guru Granth Sahib. 'Anand Karaj'—the Blissful Wedding—is solemnized by the recitation of the four wedding hymns and after each hymn is recited, the couple circumambulate, clockwise, the

Guru Granth Sahib. In the Khalsa/Sikh marriages the Guru Himself is regarded as the witness. Because of the strong tradition of family life the weddings are regarded as very special occasions and lavish festivities are mounted.

Although parents traditionally do have a decisive say in the choice of marriage partners for their children, yet it would be wrong to say that the children are condemned to an utterly closed system of arranged marriages. A much more flexible approach exists amongst the Khalsa/Sikh families.

Death is not marked by any so called 'last rite' ceremonies. However, appropriate prayers are offered for the peace of the departed soul. The Khalsa/Sikh cremate their dead.

Khalsa/Sikhs' Food habits

The vast majority of the Khalsa/Sikhs enjoy, and relish good food. They have a sweet tooth and so much of their food contains a good measure of milk, butter, curd or yogourt, chapatis and is well seasoned. These have been the traditional staple diet of the Khalsa/Sikhs. Now, they have started taking a liking to the Western food, especially fish and chips. Again, as in most other things, the Khalsa/Sikh or Panjabi curried meals are not unduly hot, but are a blend between the excessively mild and the excessively spicey. To reiterate, it must be clearly stated that there are no religious taboos about Khalsa/Sikh food except that it should be clean, fresh, wholesome and consummable by the humans.

Khalsa/Sikh 'Gurparabs' and Festival

During the year, the Khalsa/Sikh celebrate, Birth Anniversary of Guru Nanak, Vaisakhi—birth of the Khalsa, Martyrdom Day of Guru Arjan, Guru Granth Sahib Installation Day, Diwali, Guru Teg Bahadar Martrdom Day, Guru Gobind Singh's Birthday, besides others. Full details are appended.

EPILOGUE

The Sikh Gurus' charity of spirit embraced people of every nation, and their divinely-inspired, humanistic, egalitarian vision and enlightened wisdom saw the manifest Grace of the Waheguru, Almightly God, active in all souls of every religious persuasion. They selflessly worked for global peace, human happiness, the betterment of the world, goodwill amongst the Family of Waheguru, i.e., Humankind and the passionate adoration of the 'Nam' and Love of the Creator, the Waheguru Himself.

The concluding stanza of the Khalsa/Sikh congregational prayer, recited in every Gurdwara twice daily, affirms;

'Nanak Nam Chardi Kala Tere Bhane Sarbat Ka Bhala'
Nanak Lovingly Invoke the Ever-Ascendent 'NAM' of the Waheguru
By Thy Infinite Grace and Sweet Will, May the whole Humankind be Blessed

BIBLIOGRAPHY
Guru Granth Sahib: the Primary Source of Sikhism
'Sada Ithas'—The History of the Khalsa/Sikhs: Satbir Singh
The Sacred Writings of the Sikhs: Trilochan Singh and others
A History of the Sikhs: Khushwant Singh
The Spirit Born People: Prof. Puran Singh
The Gospel of the Guru Granth Sahib: Duncan Greenless
Sikhism—A Comparative Study of its Theology and Mysticism: Daljeet Singh
A History of Sikh People: Gopal Singh

CUSTOMS

Social Customs more Asian than specifically Religious.

Many social customs and attitudes in Asia have through the long process of time been given the final sanction of religious tradition—but in reality they have no reference in religious scripture, nor compulsion in moral law. They have been arrived at by the process of experience and experiment for almost twice as long as the European attempts at civilisation. This is the reason why they carry with them a subtle sense of racial superiority and why also Asians feel deep down in their hearts that the West has much to answer for.

There is an old story among the Nagas, the headhunting tribe of N.E. India, that God tried hard to make man in his own image. First he put him in the oven to cook, and burnt him. Thus the black races were created. Then God tried again and under-cooked him—this was the white race. The third time he tried—successfully this time—for man came out of the oven a nice golden brown!

Many Asians coming to the West have a golden dream of European civilisation, imbibed from years of rule from British, French, Dutch and Portuguese; from Christian schooling; from close contact with British University world, and the culture of their literature.

Living with the Britons in the raw is a great cultural shock for them also. They see the seamy side of their lives as well: perhaps the *greatest* single shock to their systems after the colour question (and *their* own sense of superiority here) is the way the British treat their elderly people. Again and again this comes up in conversation.

At the Indian village level caste and subcaste or *gotras* still influence the choice of partner but at the educated level even Muslim and Hindu are marrying each other occasionally. *Divorce* is rare—and the only ground is adultery, or infertility on the part of either partner, in which case a second marriage is allowed. However, if the reason for divorce is inability to produce children the first wife must be maintained properly and supported by the husband as a member of the family. Muslim, Hindu and Sikh societies all have a system whereby elders of the family and the village use their good offices to try and bring about reconciliation or to smooth out tensions. Because of the nature of immigration and the resultant break-up of families this force for good is sadly lacking in Britain.

In modern urban families back in Asia greater freedom of choice is being given to sons and daughters to seek out their partners in life—but always under the close guidance of the parents. This is on the whole accepted. There are some young people who rebel but it is their marriages that are more likely to founder as they run against very strong currents in society and the binding agents of interwoven family life.

The position of women causes some ambivalence of attitude. The results of social customs grown out of historical developments where women had to be protected against abduction, clash with the philosophical idea of complete equality, certainly in early Hindu thought and in Sikh social life.

However, at the city level educated women have in some instances more freedom than in the West in that domestic help is much more easily obtained and they can call on the help of many relatives also if they wish to run careers as well as homes.

Joint Family

Such an attitude arises from the gigantic strength and enclosure of their extended family system where joint households of three or four generations still live under one roof. Although this is very gradually being eroded among the educated classes by urbanisation, and the individual nuclear family such as Britons' which is becoming the pattern of much urban life, still over 80 percent of the people of India and Pakistan live in the villages—and this is where the population explosion is occurring so extremely. It will take, therefore, generations yet to change this vast area of society. And even those who have moved out of its sphere of activity still feel its influence and retain one foot in the village. There are families comprising more than 100 members living together under one roof. No child therefore ever feels neglected—even in the poorest families—and the duties and burdens of family life are shared. The isolation of Western urban life can therefore be a very great psychological shock to Asian women used to a wide-ranging network of family relationships.

The first thing an outsider notices in Asia is the moving respect for elders of the family and a welcome affectionate respect for the parents. The second is the confusing and almost unlearnable names with which each relative is designated—a different word in Urdu and Hindi is given to the grandparents on the paternal side from those on the maternal side. *Nana* is the maternal grandfather, *Dada* is the paternal grandfather. An uncle older than the father has a different name from the younger brother of a child's father. So it goes on. In Bengali there are 64 different words for various relatives!

The joint family is built up on this great cohesive sense of unity. In a continent without national insurance or a welfare state, the extended family is one great insurance policy. The eldest son carries a heavy burden of financial responsibility when the parents can no longer labour in the fields or factories. It is a moral obligation to support the old people. This is carried over in this country so that old people make far less drain on the welfare services than the indigenous old pensioners do where their own younger members have deserted them. Even individual villages take responsibility for distant kin, and unearning members of a family. This can lead to confusions for immigration officers and officials in Britain. Sometimes Asian children can quite genuinely look on a relative as a 'father', who has their total welfare in hand. This is an accepted custom in Asia, and explains why teachers who wish to see a child's parents may be visited by a distant relative instead. *Asian relatives come to stay*—and stay for months. Asians accept this, the crowding and the consequent personal inconvenience without demur.

Family property is often pooled and daughters-in-law bring their dowry wealth into the joint family. Nowadays dowries are forbidden by Indian law (the Hindu Code Bill of the 1950's). Law may legislate but social custom dies hard, and still a good deal of hard bargaining can go on before a marriage is arranged.

Dowry customs amongst Muslims are similarly extravagant though the Religion of Islam has simple traditions to its credit on the eve of marriage of a boy or a girl.

Hospitality. Another shock to both Pakistani and Indians is the diminished sense of hospitality in the West. They may not even realise that among British people themselves relationships are more formal and reticent, that they do not easily drop in on each other unannounced (nor at all times of night!), whereas they extend a very warm welcome to the stranger however unexpected he may be. *Atithi*—the Sanskrit word for guest—the stranger who comes unannounced, 'undated' is the literal meaning—is regarded as the honoured guest. This is why when any Westerner visits an Asian household they continue their overwhelming hospitality even to the point of overloading a plate with food so that it makes it very difficult either to eat it all up—or to refuse! Even on Christian festivals in India or Pakistan, Asians return the compliment by bringing gifts as well as on their own festivals.

Within the family the attitudes of Indians to *marriage and divorce* are very little different to those of Pakistanis. The arranged marriage is almost universal with perhaps nowadays a 'vetting' of each other by the young couple and a chance to withdraw if they cannot stand the sight of each other. Otherwise such marriages within their own environment and culture have proved as equally successful as the Western opposite approach. 'You fall in love, marry and repent at leisure'—says the Asian. 'We marry and then fall in love. Then there is less chance of disillusion'. Problems arise however in this country where children, especially girls, have grown up with one foot in this culture, and imbibed western ideas of personal freedom and permissiveness through primary and secondary school education. Cases of rebellion and deep tension are growing. (See *Between Two Cultures* by Dr Muhammad Anwar, a CRE publication that surveys the changing out-look on life of Asian youths in Britain). A custom that is valid in an environment where it is universally practised is very hard to enforce where other girls, the majority, are clearly seen to live entirely differently, and many uneducated Asian parents do not fully make allowance for the overwhelming pressures on their teenagers.

Strangely enough at village level where women are labourers in the fields, in road-making, in building hydro-electric schemes and dams, they also can be fairly militant and free within a given framework. Throughout the sub-Continent there is a universal respect for women, especially the mother, who enjoys a status within the home to be envied by her Western sisters. For a foreign woman too, Asia is perhaps one of the safest areas in the world in which to travel alone. In South India there is a long established matriarchal system of society where all money is passed down through the female side of the family. Here women had a long tradition of education. There have been women philosophers, warrior leaders, politicians and saints who have given the lie to the image of the retiring Asian woman totally subjected to male rule. There is no doubt that due to man-made customs Asian women have suffered the same disability as Western women socially and economically. *Purdah* is still in existence in remote areas and in some less-well educated homes. But because an Asian woman is by nature more modest and retiring it does not necessarily mean to say that she has an inferior position *within* the family structure. Her *actual* status as a mother is unquestionable and her children pay her far more attention and respect than a good many Western mothers receive.

There is the Prophet's saying to the effect that: If you are seeking Heaven look for it under mother's feet.

Because very educated Asian women are as emancipated and are holding responsible jobs in business and Government as in the West (sometimes ironically more so) this does not mean to say that they behave socially in quite the same manner as Western women. Long tradition, and even a desire to remain very modest and graceful, influences their outward mannerisms. They are not so aggressive, blatant, outspoken.

There are therefore many misunderstandings when Asian men come to the West. The new atmosphere of unisex among the British younger generation, the fact that the girls can move with total freedom, go into pubs, have open friendships between male and female *without* any emotional involvement, leaves much ground for ambiguity of understanding. 'Just being friends' is an almost unknown concept in Asia between man and woman except among the minute proportion of sophisticated elite. Open-hearted behaviour on the part of English women is therefore open to grave misunderstanding. So few Asian men have ever the chance to meet their own women on these natural terms, and can therefore hardly conceive of unemotional involvement based on purely social and mental equality of behaviour.

Caste
Caste at the village level in India is dying out very slowly. Within factories and

town life the whole pattern of rigidity is breaking more quickly. The same piped water tap in a factory, for instance, has to be used by all for drinking purposes. Even the same goes for toilets. But it is beginning to show its strength again in the political arena because of the tussle for power and personal wealth at the village level where factions on caste lines have recently proved very strong. In the towns of Pakistan and India a new system of demarcation is appearing—between the well-placed and the displaced, marking the status of families as in Victorian England. This hinders the free matrimonial choice of partners, and social gatherings. In this respect Britain is now much more democratic in attitude and social workers have found great difficulty in understanding the rigidity of social hierarchy among the Asian communities of Britian. This needs to be recognised and brought out into the open. Many British women working as voluntary helpers treat the uneducated Asian women who come to the clinics with a greater sense of respect than do their own educated classes.

Health and Food

The Hindu is much influenced from the beginning by 'Ahimsa'—non violence means non-killing. Respect for the life of all living creatures is deeply rooted in the Hindu mind. This is sometimes criticised by foreigners who raise the question of wars and the violence of partition between India and Pakistan.

Inevitably violence is part of human nature and the human condition, but the Hindu will try, unless provoked or unless a higher duty or social code is endangered, to respect the idea of Ahimsa. Killing for the sake of personal desire or satisfaction is forbidden. Therefore a great majority of orthodox Hindus eat no meat at all and are totally vegetarian to the extent even of refusing eggs as living matter, and onions as arousing passion and heating the blood, as well as because of the aesthetic sense that they smell the breath, and cause intestinal wind.

The lack of meat certainly leads to dietary deficiencies in a cold climate where the vitamin D qualities of the life-giving sun are also absent. Yet another reason for rickets and TB appearing is that the browner Asian skin protects the inner fibre cells of the body from absorbing too much sunlight. It is nature's own protection against radiation and ultra-violet rays in tropical climates. But where sun is lacking it even prevents the absorption of vitamin D from what little sun the British climate allows.

Also through lack of play outside and the fact that many Asian mothers do not venture out of doors too much, through unfamiliarity, psychological alienation and little English, children are very susceptible to respiratory diseases. Asian parents need much guidance in this respect as they do not understand how devastating the change of climate can be—living in an Asian village in an open-air life and, despite poverty, can be ironically healthier than

111

crowded conditions in our slum areas. Many instances of Asians, men and women, suffering from mental depression have come to light.

Death
Hindus cremate the dead body (unlike Muslims who bury their dead in ancestral grounds and a very few Hindu sects who bury their dead in a crosslegged posture in salt). In India, of course, cremation is done matter of factly, in the open on high pyres of sweet-smelling sandal-wood. The body is just wrapped in a simple cotton shroud, a few Sanskrit Shalokas are chanted and the ashes are collected, sometimes to be scattered in the holy river Ganges, known as Mother Ganges, or *Ganga Mata,* or at a centre of holy pilgrimage. Sometimes ashes are sent back from this country but on a whole, as death is accepted as a gateway to a new life, a renewal, in fact, the Hindu does not mind about particulars or ceremonies and has his ashes scattered naturally—in the words of the Brahmin: *'Yatrāye tatre gachhte'*—He goes to where he comes from.

The tradition of going to the Ganges of pilgrimage for religious reasons of cleansing the body and spirit is relevant to British authorities who may be seeking records of peoples' births, marriages and deaths. The majority of Hindu families at least will have recorded these with the family priests or *pandats* in the main holy cities. Family backgrounds—sometimes up to twenty generations and without mistakes—are recorded with the *pandats* even if civil authorities do not possess reliable documentation.

Names
The problem which the British generally face with the names of Indians and Pakistanis is well known. Too many Alis and Singhs have caused chaos in hospital and industrial and electoral records. The title Begum for instance is only a Muslim courtesy title for a woman. It is *not* a surname. All Sikh females use Kaur as a second name. It is *never* a surname. Registrars may be confused therefore if a Kushwant Singh comes to register his daughter as Mala Kaur. Neither Singh nor Kaur surnames as we acknowledge them. Registrars and other authorities need to ask for a forename (not a 'Christian' name), a given name (often a pen name acquired in recent generations) or baptismal name, and a family or surname. Pakistani names have been dealt with in the section on Islam.

Customary contrast among the Indus traditions differ in different parts of the country—it is like travelling through Europe, so contrasting are the strong regional and provincial cultural differences of India.

People with a fair complexion generally come from the Punjab and have a subcaste such a Puri, Sharma, Kohli, Kapur, Khosla. This is used as the surnames. The first name—corresponding to Christian name—is often based

112

on Sanskrit or the names of Hindu Gods and Goddesses or meanings of beautiful significance, certainly where girls' names are concerned. Purnima means 'night of full moon' and Kanwal means 'Lotus-eyed'. Names such as Shiv, Krishen Mahesh, Arjun, Ram Kumar (son of Rama), Narayan all derive from the names of deities and religious figures. Mostly the name consists of three parts:

> Davinder Kumar Puri
> Ajit Kumar Sharma

Kumari means 'the daughter of', and is attached at the beginning of the name of a single girl such as Raj Kumari Amrit Kaur.

In Bengal Hindu names are in the same pattern but there are many more distinctive Sens, Boses, Tagores and Rais or Roys.

From Bombay side and Gujarat district as a rule the father's name and professional title are included, as for example

Natha Lal	Bhiku Bhai	Patel
1	2	3

the first being the name of the individual, the second that of the father, the 'patel' standing for the agriculturalist, or the one who owns land. Mistry is another very familiar name for Gujaratis, meaning a mason or bricklayer, or skilled person generally.

There are a few sects who use their religion as the surname—Mahesh Kumar *Jain*. And in South India the system is even more complicated. There are usually three names, and very elongated at that. Two brothers will have different names as surnames because in India these are their personal names which they use as surnames, dropping their caste names when they come here—and in the middle will be the village name—thus Sunderaraja Khottandaram Iyengar—will be using the first name as his proper name, the middle name for his village, the last name as his caste name. The last name may therefore be dropped and this person be known as Mr Sunderaraja. His brother may be Narasinha Kottandaram Iyengar and be known as Mr Narasinha.

Marathi names can often be picked out by the ending Kar, such as Mulgaokar, Karendikar, or Ambedkar. These people usually come from Bombay side.

Such minor details illustrate the wide spectrum of custom, tradition and behaviour within Asian society. Too many Westerners make the mistake of stereotyping all Asians as one people without recognising that perspectives and attitudes are not only dependent of class, education, urban and rural backgrounds but also on ethnic groups, language and consequently regional culture. In a geographical land-mass as vast as the Indian sub-Continent nations exist within nations. One state alone in India is larger than the entire United Kingdom and has over 90 million inhabitants. This is Uttar Pradesh. There are sixteen major languages plus English spoken in India and eight major religions (Hinduism, Buddhism, Jainism, Zoroastrianism—Parsees, Judaism, Christianity, Islam and Sikhism in order of historic emergence).

And as far as culture goes, a Kenyan or Ugandan Asian may be very different from a Punjabi or Gujarati Indian or Pakistani from the mainland. Differentiation has also to be made between a Punjabi Indian and a Punjabi Pakistani as well as between an Indian Punjabi Muslim, Sikh or Hindu where attitudes again have different emphasis. A Mirpuri Pakistani is not at all the same in his thinking as a Karachi Sindhi. A Madrasi and a Bengali may only be united by a common heritage of Indian secular thought constantly evolving from the ever-replenishing reservoir of a multi-religious, multi-ethnic, multi-cultural society which has been experimenting along these lines for twice as long as the Christian civilization.

Face structures, dress, food, symbols and gestures reflect the outer manifestations of this incredibly diverse inner life of the sub-Continent. It is this diversity that is slowly seeping into British sub-soil through the recent influx from immigration.

The immigration is, however, too often seen exclusively in the context of a problem area. Of course rapid transfer of people in a jumbo-jet age and large-scale concentration in some areas does create dislocation, physical as well as psychological. Even the mobility of newly arrived people, and their to-ing and fro-ing to the Asian sub-Continent for marriages or the visiting of relatives (made possible in an age of cheap charter flights) may defer real indentification with the new country of abode. For the native British also this wave of immigration is somewhat different from that of previous history in that the new citizens come from civilisations outside of the Christian and Jewish framework. Problems there are. Children growing up stradling two cultures face very real inner conflicts, and confusions of principle and norms of behaviour. Mothers not only face isolation in communication but an extra dimension of alienation from husbands and children coming under more direct influence of indigenous British society, itself undergoing radical changes not only in degree but also in kind. Rural people from the traditional hierarchical societies of Asia could not have encountered the British at a more complex time. Fifty years ago British societies, based on class, status, respectability, the outer form rather than the inner essence, would have been more absorbative of rural Asian family values.

In some ways the very fact that a new settler is on the defensive in a more hostile climate of opinion than the one he has left (although this is not always so) is conducive to his becoming more traditional in attitude, more ingrown in thinking, more aware of religious principles. Just as the English abroad remain more English that those at home, the same can be said for Asians who may have settled here long enough not to know *by experience* rather than by intellect the rapid changes now going on in society in the main-stream culture of the Asian mainland. The younger generations are more aware because of their 'grapevines' and also because they can read the English magazines coming out of Asia. This is bound to lead to tensions compounded by our own rapid changes in a sophisticated urban society. It is, however, remarkable how resilient the younger Asian generation are, almost naturally embracing a double identity. Asian at home with some Western Innovations, British in the wider society beyond the home. In an increasingly mobile world this may well be the pattern of the future for young people everywhere who are on the move.

Yet subtle changes are already making themselves felt even in the most traditional Pakistani family who by the very nature of a more authoritarian culture may be said to be the last to change. Women are beginning to learn English out of necessity: the sheer inconvenience of having to rely permanently upon their children for the most intimate of interpretings makes the step inevitable. And these self-same women are divesting themselves of baggy shalwars either under the influence of their daughters or by what they see other women doing. Crimplene suits are now worn for shopping expeditions if not yet when visiting fellow Asians and relatives.

But beyond all this, on a wider canvas, the creative world of possibilities and opportunities exists for enrichment of British common citizenship and the overall society. Cross-fertilisation of cultures have always created ferment in artistic endeavour and intellectual ideas. Personal identity and common identity can create a multi-cultural society of real talent and potential, a palimpsest of many layers. This characteristic has marked Asian thinking and living for at least four thousand years. It gave the sub-Continent of India a universalistic approach to life and a tolerant attitude to other religions, despite recent political exacerbations.

It is time to acknowledge that immigration is not a one-way street to selfish personal aggrandisement and security. There are values and positive enrichment to be contributed by newcomers, and not only in the area of economic national wealth. There is much to learn from the steadfast values of Asian family life; much to reach out to in school life in new books and curriculum and stories from Asian literature to capture the imagination. Libraries have a great opportunity to enlarge our knowledge of these civilisations. Sport, theatre, evolving social attitudes, all in their own ways stand to gain from the new Asian perspectives that are in Britain once we recognise the full force of the possibilities and the opportunities in which they seek fulfilment.

ASIAN FESTIVALS

Political Festivals

January 26th	Indian Republic Day
March 23rd	Pakistan Republic Day
March 26th	Bangladesh Independence Day
August 14th	Independence Day.........Pakistan
August 15th	Independence Day.........India

(these two days celebrate the ending of the British Raj and the handing over of Independence to the two sovereign republics in 1947).

Religious and cultural festivals

January 19th (1981) *Eid-Milad-un-Nabi* – the Prophet Muhammad's Birthday (August 20, 570 CE – 12 **Rabi-ul-Awwal** in the Muslim Calendar), the most important day in the history of Islam. A series of lectures and discourses are arranged in the mosques or other centres on the sacred life of the Prophet and development of Islam. Children have stories depicting his love and care for his followers narrated to them.

March 2nd (1981) *Holi* – the Hindu festival, a Bacchanalia of fertility and spring, celebrated in Northern and Central India but not in Bengal or the South. It goes back to very ancient times, to the mythology of the cruel King, Harna Kashyap, and his real-son Prahlad whom he hated because he was religious. One day he decided to kill Prahlad for worshipping the Divine, instead of himself – and tried to enlist the help of his sister, Holika. She had been blessed by the Devas and could not be touched by fire, so that when Kashyap lit a bonfire to destroy Prahlad (whom he had sat on Holika's lap in the bonfire), Holika was burnt up and Prahlad escaped, untouched by the flames. Hindus now celebrate this as one more triumph of the forces of Good over Evil.
Symbolically it is the Indian harvest thanksgiving in a country-side which can support three crops a year if properly tilled. The spring wheat is harvested at this time and there is much singing and merry-making.

The throwing of red powder and water over anyone in sight up to midday of Holi expresses the intoxication and lack of inhibition similar to the Mardi Gras of Latin countries before Lent, and the Greek Dionysian rites. By the orthodox Hindu calendar the Lord Krishna returns on this day to Gokul, the temple city of Brindaban, near Delhi, playing his flute and dancing with the Gopis or milkmaids. One of the cow-herds dancing for joy smeared the Gopis with turmeric powder mixed in milk so in turn they took kum-kum powder (the red decorative cosmetic powder) and sprinkled it on the men.

Nowadays it is a day for wild childish pranks.

March 2nd (1981)   *Holla* - is similar festival to Holi, quite popular in the North of India. Guru Gobind Singh provided an alternative celebration for the Sikhs, a three-day fair held at Anandpur Sahib, beginning on the eve of Holi. Tents are pitched and stalls erected. Crowds assemble for a variety of activities, singing, talks about Sikhism and political conferences. On the Hola day of the Hola itself there are exhibitions of horse riding, tournaments, and athletic competition, for Sikhism has always placed importance upon physical health, and there is much ribaldry and good humour.

April 13th (1981)   *Baisakhi* – the first day of the Sikh and Hindu New Year commemorating the founding of the Khalsa, the society of the pure. In several parts of Northern India it heralds the advent of a new fiscal year. To the masses it means the beginning of the new Bikrami Samit and to the farmer rewards for winter toil.

To Indians in general and to Punjabis in particular it brings back memories of the dark day of Jallianwala Bagh when General Dwyer's troops fired on a crowd of Indian freedom fighters gathered in this enclosed square in Amritsar. Since that day this festival has also been remembered as Martyrs Day.

For the Sikhs this day has special significance Guru Amar Das – the third Guru – made it one of the annual gatherings of the Sikhs, the other being Diwali, so that the Sikhs would retain their own celebrations rather than Hindu ones at the time when the Sikh religion was still in its infancy. The day is commemorated by administering Sikh baptism (the amrit) to those who wish to take serious religious vows or to re-enter the faith after re-growing their hair.

There is much festivity in Punjabi villages, melas, cattle contests in drawing the Persian wheel, and bhangra dancing where young Sikh men dance on an upturned ghará or earthenware pot *on top of* another Sikh's head.

May   *Buddha Purnima* – Celebration of the birth of the Lord Buddha more than 2,500 years ago.

July 4th (1981)   *Ramadhan* – (sometimes spelled *Ramazan* from the Arabic word *Ramaz,* meaning 'burning', the middle summer month of the Muslim year) is the period of disciplined continuous fasting which lasts 28-30 days from the sighting of one new moon to the next. The first sighting takes place 14 days after the festival *Shab-e-Barat* on the night of the full moon when prayers are said to be especially efficacious. Muslims believe that on the night of *Shab-e-Barat* God registers the actions of men and dispenses their fate according to their deeds as they stand at the moment.

In really traditional families if the new moon cannot be seen because of the weather, the joyous celebration of Eid is celebrated the next day. There is an especial élan felt at seeing the rising of the slender crescent in the blue/black sky of the East and people go outside on rooftops to catch a glimpse when the final fast is broken and heart-warming cries of *Eid Mubarak* – Happy *Eid* – are cried out as people embrace each other, and release comes from the patient but increasingly draining foregoing of food and liquid and smoking. It is also a release for housewives who throughout this month, no matter how tired, have to rise about 5 am to make tea and a light meal before fasting begins at sunrise. The main meal is taken at sunset and in many a Muslim home in England, on the English mantelshelf of a breakfast room stands the Urdu calendar with each day's sunset demarcated, and paragraphs of exhortation not to lie, swear, think evil of others, etc. In the winter months as the sun sets earlier by 2 or 3 minutes the fasting period lessens but in English summers in the long days the periods will be even more excessive than in the East where sunset is earlier in the tropics.

August 2nd (1981)   *Eid-ul-Fitr* — the great day of celebration when
Muslims the world over give thanks for coming through
the strenuous month of *Ramadhan*. On this day,
equivalent to Christmas, special spiced dishes are cooked, decorations are hung and families reunite and have a
happy time. *Eid* means 'rejoicing' and *Fitr* 'charity'. In
the morning men take a bath and go to the mosque for
prayers. Two or three days are taken off from work. In
the UK Muslims now begin to feel the lack of real
celebration on the correct day, and the air of festivity
that enriches these great moments of festival in Islamic
countries. They are representing to the authorities for a
holiday off work on this festive day.

August 29th (1981)   *Janamashtami* — The Nativity Festival of Lord
Krishna. This is held on the eighth day of the dark part
of the month during the lunar waning. His birth place
was the prison of a tyrant and legend has it that (like the
birth of the Prophet Moses) he was rescued from prison
by the swopping of babies.

The Lord Krishna — the 'Blue God' — is symbolic of
too much to the average Indian Hindu. He is perhaps
most the symbol of the eternal God who drinks the
whole poison of evil in the universe which turned him
this colour to protect mankind from such evil. In Sanskrit it is said: 'Karshti sai Krishn' — 'That who attracts
is Krishna'. A myriad legends are woven around this incarnation of the Lord Vishnu. He is the child Krishna
who plays naughty pranks on everyone, and the
amorous lover, the Hindu Cupid who steals the clothes
of the Gopis while they are bathing in the river Jumna;
he is the heroic warrior and philosopher of the epic,
Mahabharata; he is the diplomat who always champion-
ed the cause of justice; he epitomises to orthodox Hindus the social and ethical values embedded in their long
philosophical scriptures. He is, above all, beloved, not
being remote or ascetic like Vishnu or Shiva. Usually he
is depicted wandering in the mystic woods, playing
glorious melodies from his ever-present flute.
Janamashtami or Krishanashtami falls at midnight, the
time of the birth. It is celebrated mainly in North and
Central India, and especially by the Gujarati Patels and
the Maharashtrians from Bombay side who have come

to Britain. Small devas of the Lord Krishna are on many English mantelpieces in this country. Back in India men and women fast on the previous day and after the birth time they eat sweetmeats after first offering them to the image of God. Usually they do this in the temple where they spend the whole night singing Kirtans and bhajans till midnight. Then they place the image of the baby Krishna in a flower-bedecked cradle and all night they celebrate his birth.

September 1st (1981) *Ganesh Chaturthi* – Ganesh, the elephant God of prosperity and good fortune, son of Shiva and Parvati, is a favourite of children and students. He presides over the lintel of doorways in Hindu homes to ward away evil, or faces the open door from inside a room to bring good fortune to those who enter.

This festival is celebrated with great colour and aplomb in Bombay and Maharashtra for more than 10 days. A clay image is made of Ganesh or Ganapathi and is worshipped with music, feasting and dancing. Cultural programmes are organised. People go visiting and on the last day the image of Ganesh is taken out in procession, with bands and music, and immersed in the river or the sea.

September/October *Ram Navami* – The ninth day of the fight between the historical King Rama of Ayodhya, and Ravana, the Demon King of Lanka (Ceylon).

October 9th (1981) *Durga Puja* – is the Bengali Dussehra Festival, in honour of the Goddess Durga, the female principle of Energy (the Shakti) and the mother of the world, earth, fertility. Durg means 'castle' in Sanskrit, implying the honouring of the Mother who protects all her children from external dangers just as the fortress castle does. Rama invoked the help of Durga in overcoming the demon-king Ravana.

Statues of the Goddess are made in the suburbs of big cities by colonies of Bengalis, each trying to outdo the other in the elaborate papier mache representations of the ten-armed Goddess, each hand holding the symbolic weapons of destruction (cf. Zimmer, H, *Myths and Symbols in Indian Art and Civilization,* Harper Torchbooks). On the fourth day after worship with fire in front of the deity and physical feats of dancing by young men to test their prowess, the statues are immersed in the waters of a holy tank (pool) or river as the sun sets. New clothes are worn and gifts exchanged.

Navratri – The Festival of Nine Nights (Nau = nine, raat = night in Hindi) leading up to Dussehra (Das = ten) is unique to Gujarat and celebrated with great verve and gaiety. It has indeed been called fiesta time. All the young girls get dressed up in saris which they do not normally wear until the late teens or marriage. Their hair is decked in flowers. Older married ladies, fathers, brothers, sisters, all go to the temple and dedicate themselves to the Mother Goddess Durga locally known as Amba, or affectionately Ambaji. Often the Goddess is placed in a miniature 'mandap' or canopy structure fashioned like a tiny temple. For hours the women and girls move anticlockwise in a large circle dancing the 'garba' while singers pour out verse after verse of long ballads on themes of chivalry, the love of Krishna, Radha, and the Gopis, or miraculous events, magic and miracles never being far from Hindu belief in Gujarati culture. Even commentary on local customs of society are incorporated in these ballads which enables an oral tradition to pass the culture on from one generation to another.

Men and women can dance together in the circle, keeping rhythm with a drum and attractively lacquered sticks. In Gujarat itself people snake their way through the streets, ending the garba (if it is danced by women) or garbi (if it is danced by men in Saurashtra) with increasing speed and vigour.

Garba is derived from the Sanskrit word garbha – womb, the earthen pot carved out in designs of holes with a lamp placed in it, symbolising embryonic life. During Navratri women carry these pots on their heads and sing praises of Ambaji. Even in England Gujaratis gather together in their hundreds to celebrate with dancing, singing, the arti or light worship through the nine nights bringing colour and joy into grey autumnal evenings.

October 9th (1981)   *Eid-ul-Adha:* The moveable Muslim commemoration of The Prophet Ibrahim's offer to sacrifice his son, Ishmael, to the glory of God. The Prophet Ibrahim's

121

family were in Mecca to look after the Holy place of the *Kaaba*. This lunar date is commemorated a little earlier each year, working backwards through the Western calendar (see Islam section for full details). Goats and sheep are sacrificed and sold to raise money for orphanages and scholarships for the poor. This *Eid* concentrates the mind on the needs of poverty. Charitable institutions are set up with the money contributed. Families invite guests to dinner and there are huge congregational prayers in the mosques. Cattle fairs are held with great colour and noise and festivity. Muslims in Britain are requesting this day to be declared a public holiday as applicable to Muslims.

October 8th (1981) *Dussehra* – Again of unfixed date depending on the full moon. This, one of the greatest Hindu festivals celebrated universally by all Indians, follows immediately upon Ramnavami and is described in the Hinduism section.

It is terminated after 10 days of enactment of the Rama-Sita epic on open *maidans* by the autumn Festival of Lights.

October 27th (1981) *Diwali or Deepawali* – The Hindu festival symbolic of the forces of good over evil. On this dark night the Goddess Lakshmi, personification of Good Fortune and Prosperity, visits only those homes that are lit by the lights of many lamps – usually the saucer-shaped earthenware deepas filled with coconut oil and rolled cotton wicks. Woe betide the house enshrouded in darkness. This is a beautiful festival with houses and humble mud huts alike flickering in the light of thousands of such lamps.

This is also the day when a majority of business communities terminate the fiscal year and open new ledgers on the morning after Diwali. It also commemorated the welcome home to Rama after 14 years of exile and his coronation as the King of the Northern Kingdom of Ayodhya. Guru Ram Das, 4th Guru, laid the foundation stone of the Golden Temple, Darbar Sahib, at Amritsar, on this day. The Temple is profusely illuminated and the concourse linked with flickering lights, so becoming one of the most beautiful of Diwali celebrations in India, a mixture of Hindu and Sikh traditions.

*November 11th
(1981)*

Guru Nanak's Birthday, the founder of the Sikh faith and the first of the ten Gurus. This birthday is fixed again according to the lunar month. In 1969, the 500th anniversary of the Guru's birth in 1469, the day fell on November 23rd.

Preceding the festival, Sikhs undertake an akhand pāth, reading of the Holy Book non-stop. On the day of the festival, the Granth Sahib is taken out on a float under a canopy and huge crowds of Sikhs gather, especially in Old Delhi, throwing marigolds into the crowd as blessing. Amritsar, Taran Taran, and Anandpur, sacred cities to the Sikhs, also celebrate in style.

*December 25th
(1981)*

Birthday of Quaide-e-Azam Muhammad Ali Jinnah, the founder of the Islamic Republic of Pakistan.

*January 12th
(1982)*

Sikh celebration of Guru Gobind Singh's birthday.

Basant – another moveable date of the Indian Punjabi Spring festival when yellow turbans and saris and new long skirts *(lehengas,* sometimes 15 yards at the hem) are donned. Yellow is the spring colour, reflected in the open plains of the Punjab in the *sarson* – the mustard-like vegetable which flames with yellow flowers. This is also the colour of bravery (just the opposite of the Western idiom) and fertility. This is the symbol of the yellow in the Indian flag going back to Rajput traditions. Fairs or melas are held and especially music concerts. There is a Punjabi saying: *'Ai basant pale urant'* – when Basant comes, the cold flies away.

SOME USEFUL ADDRESSES

The following can be contacted for further information on the subjects dealt with in this book.

Hinduism
Raja Yoga Centre
(Ishvarya Vishwa-Vidyalaya)
98 Tennyson Road
London NW6
Tel. 01-328 2478

Ramakrishna Vedanta Centre
54 Holland Park
London W11
Tel. 01-727 4010

Vedic Mission (Arya Samaj)
London
14 Penderel Road
Hounslow
Middlesex

Islam
Dar-ul-Ehan Publications
252 Almondbury Bank
Almondbury
Huddersfield HD5 8EL
Contact: Dr M Iqbal
Tel. 0484-26197

Islamic Cultural Centre
25 Park Street
Aston
Birmingham B6 5SH
Contact: Mr B A Awan
Tel. 021-327 1281

The Islamic Foundation
223 London Road
Leicester LE12 1ZE
Contact: K J Murrand
Tel. 0533-70025

Islamic Cultural Centre
146 Park Road
London NW8
Contact: Dr Zaki Badawi
Tel. 01-723 7611-3

Muslim Education Consutlative
Committee
2A Bowyer Road
Saltley
Birmingham B8 1AT
Contact: Lt Col M A Khan
Tel. 021-440 3083

Muslim Educational Trust
130 Stroud Green
London N4 3RZ
Tel. 01-272 8502

Union of Muslim Organizations of
UK and Eire
30 Baker Street
London W1M 2DS
Contact: Dr Syed A Pasha
Tel. 01-229 0538

Dar-ul-Ehsan Centre 273
8 Bruce Grove
Watford WD2 5AG
Contact: Haji M Ramzan
Tel. 0923-45376

Northern Council of Gurdwaras and
Sikh Organisations
Britannia Buildings Portland Street
Bradford BD5 0DW
West Yorkshire
Chairman: Sardar A K Singh

Sikhism
Sikh Studies Research Foundation
UK
32 Gledholt Road
Gledholt
Huddersfield HD1 4HP
West Yorkshire
Director-General: Sardar Arjan
Kirpal Singh
Tel. 0484 21839

The Sikh Cultural Society of Great
Britain
88 Mollison Way Edgware Middlesex
Greater London HA8 5QW
Tel. 01-952 1215

Information Secretary: Mr. A. S.
Chhatwal
Guru Nanak Charitable Trust UK
Britannia Buildings Portland Street
Bradford BD5 0DW
West Yorkshire
Secretary-General: Mr M S Bussan,
JP

Federation of Sikh Organisations UK
19 Douglas Road Surbiton
Surrey KT6 7RZ
Co-ordinating Secretary: Harcharan
Singh
Tel. 01-399 0942

Miscellaneous
R E Centre
West London Institute of
  Higher Education
Lancaster House
Borough Road
Isleworth
Middlesex TW7 5DU
Tel. 01-560 5991

R E Centre
Westhill College of Education
Selly Oak
Birmingham B29 6LL
Tel. 021-472 1563

Islamic Centre
Central College
Selly Oak
Birmingham B29 6LE
Tel. 021-472 4231

R E Centre
College of Ripon and York St John
York
Tel. 0904 56771

R E Centre
Homerton College
Cambridge CB2 2PH
Tel. 0223 44122

University of Lancaster
Project on Religious Education
Cartmel College
Bailrigg
Lancaster
Tel. Lancaster 65202

Standing Conference on
 Inter-Faith Dialogue in Education
c/o World Congress of Faiths
23 Norfolk Square
London W2 1RU
Tel. 01-723 9820

Information and Advisory Officer
SHAP Working Party on
 World Religions in Education
Borough Road College
Isleworth
Middlesex TW7 5DU
Tel. 01-560 5991

North-West Regional Inter-Faith
 Conference
Edge Hill College of Higher
 Education
St Helens Road
Ormskirk
Lancashire

Dar-ul-Ehsan Centre 461
1029 Stockport Road
Levanshulme
Manchester M19 2TB
Contact: Dr M A Zafar
Tel. 061-442 8861

Christianity
Friends Community Relations
 Committee
Friends House
Euston Road
London NW1 2BJ
Tel. 01-387 3601

Community & Race Relations Unit
British Council of Churches
10 Eaton Gate
London SW1 9BT
Tel. 01-730 9611

Church Missionary Society
157 Waterloo Road
London SE1 8UU
Tel. 01-928 8681

National Society
Church House
Dean's Yard
Westminster SW1
Tel. 01-222 9011

Division of Social Responsibility of
 the Methodist Church
1 Central Buildings
London SW1
Tel. 01-930 2638

Westminster Religious Education
 Centre
209 Old Marylebone Road
London NW1 5QT
Tel. 01-402 6353/4

Missions and Other Faiths Committee
United Reformed Church
86 Tavistock Place
London WC1H 9RT
Tel. 01-837 7661

Relgious Education Council of England and Wales
123 Green End Road
Hemel Hempstead HP1 1RT
Contact: James Thompson
Tel. 0442 54845

INDEX

130

NOTES

NOTES

NOTES

NOTES